To Jenna,

a true power. How the road to success.

Your wishes come true. Much many blessings, and Peace from,

"The Genie" Kaheal Shropes

A Blueprint for the Perfect Life

101 Secrets to Live the Life of Your Dreams

"The Genie" Kabral Sharpe

iUniverse, Inc.
Bloomington

A Blueprint for the Perfect Life
101 Secrets to Live the Life of Your Dreams

iUniverse
1663 Liberty Drive
Bloomington, IN 47403
www.iuniverse.com
1-800-Authors (1-800-288-4677)

ISBN: 978-1-4759-6096-9 (sc)
ISBN: 978-1-4759-6097-6 (hc)
ISBN: 978-1-4759-6098-3 (e)

Library of Congress Control Number: 2012921073

Printed in the United States of America

iUniverse rev. date: 4/11/2013

As a complimentary gift to you that goes
with this purchase, we are offering you your
"Wish Fulfilled" coaching session. See appendix A
for details at the end of the book.

This book is dedicated to my mother Maya. Everything I am in some way or the other relates back to you, either in how you have taught me, encouraged me, or simply modeled for me how to be. Without you I would have never created this book, or my company Inner Access. I am able to serve and live my life's purpose because of you. Thank you for being my inspiration and one of my greatest sources of strength and vision. You always have been and continue to be right there for me. For that I am forever grateful.

Contents

Special Thanks

I would like to give a special thanks to the following people. To my incredible wife, Nikki, who is the glue that holds it all together for our family and the foundation that helps to keep me grounded. You make me want to be the absolute best I can be. To my brilliant son, Isaiah, who fills my life with so much joy and purpose. To my exquisite daughter Zoe for taking my life from good to great. To my coach James Murphy, aka ("Merlin The Magician,") who always keeps me on track no matter what the goal and without whom this book simply would not have happened. To Maya Sharpe aka ("The Doc,") for being such an outstanding Creative Director for Inner Access, for being the back bone of the company, and for designing the cover of this book. You simply have the golden touch. To my phenomenal father, Calvin Sharpe, aka ("Pop,") who has given me my edge in life and set the standard for how to continually grow and achieve excellence. To my miraculous grandmother Alberta Hall, who instilled in me the core values of what is most important in life. To my supremely generous stepmother Jan Jones aka ("Grand J,") who has always made sure that I have experienced the best that life has to offer. To my sisters Stevie Sharpe Jones and Adrienne Jones aka ("The Movie Maker,") who epitomize spunk, fun, and heart in my life. To my other sister Diane Chung, aka ("D,") aka ("The World's Greatest Naturopath,") for inspiring me just by shining your light and being a living example of what is possible. To my In-laws

Lorna Phillips ("Mom,") Neville Phillips ("The Boss,") and Wendy Phillips aka ("DJ Wen Wen,") you are simply the greatest in-laws anyone could ever ask for. To my brothers Roman Martinez ("The Latin Jazz All Star,") Jeremy Conley ("JC,") Dino Cuzzolino ("Mr. Sunshine,") and Ed Blunt ("EB,") with whom I have had some of the greatest times of my life and with whom I have also experienced some of the greatest support in my life. To Alex Stark for being ("The Michael Jordan of Feng Shui") and always knowing exactly what to do next. To Ms. Kathleen Karter for being such a pivotal part of my support team and giving the greatest guidance. To my web designer Bob Kamp for your tremendous expertise and support with taking Inner Access to the next level. You are ("The Man.") To T. Harv Eker, Tony Robbins, Wayne Dyer, Brian Tracy, Les Brown, Jack Canfield, Matt Morris, and Julia Cameron for being my greatest mentors in the field of self-development. To Christian Mickelsen for all of your extraordinary game changing expertise. To Kieron Sweeney for consistently giving me the greatest encouragement. To Grand Master Alan Lee and Master Oswald Rivera for giving me the gift of kung fu. To my gurus Baba Muktananda and Swami Chidvilasananda for giving me the tools to experience my Source. To Jonnine Deloatch aka ("Nini,") for seeing the greatness in me from the start. To Amy McHargue for your sweet patience and support with the publishing process. To Narinder Randawe for always keeping things so organized. To Dr. Thomas Spiridellis for always keeping everything in alignment. To Dr. Pankaj Naram for the gift of ayurvedic medicine and your years of life changing support. To Sherlyn Pang Luedtke aka ("The Amazing Sherlyn,") for being such a pivotal part of Inner Access as the lead trainer and Self-Empowerment Coach. You really are Amazing. To Cara Landes aka ("Superwoman,") Julie Polito aka ("The DreamMaker,") and Byron Van Pelt aka ("The Jetsetter,") for being such important parts of our incredible coaching team. Individually you all are awesome and together we are unstoppable. (Avengers Assemble!!!) To Omar Sharpe ("The Lyrical Miracle,") April McNeil ("The Bionic Woman,") Alexis Parrin ("Supermodel,") Kristoph Matthews ("007,") Adam Lipson ("Cut Creator,") Kristy Mercker ("Wonder Woman,") and all the other incredible clients of Inner Access for giving me the outlet to contribute and live my purpose. You are living proof of the power of this work. To my beloved ancestors for laying the ground work for my life. And to all my other family, friends, teachers, and business partners, who have meant so much. You know who you are.

The Genie's Top Ten

1. The Power of Your Word #17
2. Meditation #84
3. Visualization #56
4. Affirmations #69
5. Purpose #90
6. Responsibility #2
7. Fun #19
8. Teamwork #86
9. Gratitude #4
10. Love #101

#1   Release Your Past

Release your past. So often, and in so many ways, the past hinders us. We don't attempt certain things because they did not work in the past. We mentally limit ourselves because we struggled with something in the past and now assume it will be that way if we try it again. We give ourselves and other people very disempowering labels because of past experiences and interactions. Our old ways of being are so ingrained in us that we don't even realize they are running our lives in most cases.

An example of this dynamic could be a time when you were in a relationship and someone mistreated you, and you still carry around the anger and hurt from that incident. Another example could possibly be when there was a period in your life when financially you just couldn't seem to manage all of your bills and expenses, and you created a conclusion in your mind that you were just not good with money. These types of incidents cripple you because you have made up stories about what they mean to the point that you are paralyzed with fear and feelings of unworthiness.

What if you didn't have a past? What if you could actually release from your mind any old, conditioned ways of thinking that prevent you from realizing your highest self? Tony Robbins said, "The past does not equal the future unless you live there." Imagine if you could free yourself from this trap forever. What would your life be like then? The possibilities would be limitless. In essence, it would be like driving your car and taking the emergency brake off. You would be able to move much faster, easier, and smoother on your journey toward realizing any of your intentions. Simply put, your life would be much better.

ACTION STEPS FOR RELEASING YOUR PAST

1. Approach today with a totally fresh, new attitude. Imagine that you are writing a movie and you are the star. Answer the following questions: What qualities would you have? How would you walk and talk? How would you handle challenges?

2. What ideal characteristics would you embody? When you are clear about them, play the role.

3. As you go through your day, whenever you notice yourself saying "I can't do that" or "I tried that before" or "I know how this person is going to react," just say to yourself, "Oh, that's the past," and get back into your new character. This may be somewhat challenging, but experiment and have fun with it. When you do this enough, you will notice that the old patterns have no more control over you, and it is easier for you to live powerfully.

#2   Responsibility

Responsibility. Your life is where it is because of the choices you have made. This is not a cause to blame yourself for all that is missing but, rather, an opportunity to understand just how much control you have. There is so much influence that you possess in creating your destiny. "Every action creates a reaction." When you take full responsibility for what shows up in your life, you are empowered. You are no longer just experiencing circumstances but are instead harnessing your power. By assuming full responsibility for what shows up in your world, you are much more conscious of your thoughts, words, and actions. As a result you will have a great deal more influence over your outcomes.

When you take on this mind-set, there is no room to play the role of the victim. Owning your part in creating your reality is the first step to finding the adjustments that need to be made. Otherwise, you will always think that your success lies outside of yourself. This mind-set is problematic because it totally gives away your power. This is a victim's way of thinking because you no longer have any control over what happens to you. When you have no control, you are a victim of circumstance. You must understand that you already have everything you need inside of you to realize the dreams you envision.

In order to be successful in anything, you must constantly be making adjustments. Quite often these adjustments are mental and emotional as well as physical. As Tony Robbins said, "You either need to change your process, your procedure, or both." Regardless of the kind of adjustment, once it is made, your results will vary. You will then need to make adjustments again based on those new results. This process continues over and over again until you achieve your desired outcome. However, you can never get to this place until you acknowledge how your way of being has gotten you to where you are now. Successful people fully own their role in creating their lives. This is not always a fun thing to do, and it is definitely not the way we are conditioned to think. Yet it is by far the most rewarding way to live because it enables you to embrace your power and design your life. Of course there are some situations which will be beyond your control, but in most cases you have a great deal of input if you just look to see how you can create your circumstances.

ACTION STEPS FOR RESPONSIBILITY

1. Practice taking full responsibility for every area of your life.

2. With each challenging situation that occurs, ask yourself, "How did I create this in my life?" Was it your thoughts, feelings, actions, or all of the above?

3. Then ask yourself, "What do I want, and how can I use my present circumstances to help me realize my intention?"

#3   The Power of Influence

The power of influence is a great gift. It means you have the ability to affect your surroundings and the people in your environment. There are a number of things you can do to deepen your connection to others and increase your influence. Yet there are three main principles to practice in order to have powerful influence. First, bear in mind that whatever state you are in mentally and emotionally rubs off on others. It has often been said that "enthusiasm is contagious." The same is true of anger. Emotions are simply a form of energy, and energy affects everyone whether it is high or low. If you want to have a positive effect on someone, be in a positive state. The mere transference of energy will lift their spirits and have them be more open to you. This is especially important to be aware of if you are in negotiations of any kind.

Second, engage in the practice of mirroring. When you mirror someone's body language, gestures, and even speech patterns, they will naturally feel more connected to you even if they don't know why. Mirroring naturally strengthens your rapport with people. You do not have to mirror them exactly, or even for a long time. However, if you do it enough, and you do it from the beginning of the interaction, then when you return back to your normal rhythm, they will most likely follow your lead because they will feel that you are like them and they will want to stay connected to you. This mirroring technique is called pacing.

Third, if you want to influence someone, be a true friend to them. Take a sincere interest in what they find important. Really listen to what they have to say. Establish a rapport with the person before you need something from them. This lets them know that you are not trying to use them and conveys the message that you genuinely care about them.

If you practice these three principles, you will notice your connections to people deepening and your personal influence strengthening. Remember, success in any field requires the assistance of others, so expand your field of influence starting now.

ACTION STEPS FOR EXPERIENCING YOUR POWER OF INFLUENCE

1. Practice generating enthusiasm when you speak to others and make sure to be in a peak state before important interactions.

2. Practice pacing as you mirror the people you are communicating with so that your voice and gestures enable you to create a deeper connection with them.

3. Be a true friend first. Listen to the needs of the person, and be specific with how what you are involved in applies to them.

#4 Gratitude

Gratitude. Most of us have less of it than we realize. The vast majority of people spend more time focusing on the negative and what is wrong with their lives than all that is right. There is a saying that goes "Enlightened people give thanks for what normal people take for granted." We have so much to be thankful for. There is so much more going right in your life than there is going wrong in most cases. True wealth has to include gratitude. If a person has a lot of material wealth but no gratitude then they are emotionally poor. Therefore, in order to have both, you must develop an attitude of gratitude. The more you appreciate your blessings, the more you enjoy your life. The dictionary definition of appreciation is "to increase the value of." In other words you elevate the value of anything that you are grateful for simply by appreciating it. Also, the more you are grateful, the more the universe brings prosperity your way.

When you are in a state of gratitude, your mind is contemplating all the abundance that exists in your life. As this happens, you become a magnet for more abundance. This is how the universal law of attraction plays out. Put another way, "what you think about expands," "like attracts like," "water seeks its own level." The bottom line is the more you can generate this feeling, the happier you will be and the more you will find new blessings popping up in your life.

ACTION STEPS FOR EXPERIENCING GRATITUDE

1. As you start your day, think about at least ten things that you totally appreciate in your world. It could be something as simple as your ability to walk or see, but whatever it is, acknowledge it, and then give thanks for its existence. If you want to deepen this experience, just think of how you would feel if these things that you appreciate no longer existed in your life. This will enhance your mood and help to start your day off on the right foot.

2. As you proceed through your day, give thanks for each occurrence, no matter what it is. Create the habit of saying "that's great" with each incident and search for the reasons why.

3. Before you go to bed write down and give thanks for each new blessing that you experienced in your life that day, no matter what form it took. These blessings may come in the form of material gifts, quality time with people, personal accomplishments, or any other kinds of successes from that particular day.

4. Pay close attention to how this attitude of gratitude shifts your mental state by making you happier, positively impacts your day by making you more effective, gives you more energy, and attracts even more abundance and blessings to be grateful for.

#5 Leadership

Leadership. In order to get into the top 10 percent in your field, you have to become a leader. Leaders have very specific characteristics that set them apart. These qualities are traits that all people can develop in themselves. These traits are not necessarily easy to acquire, but through steady application they can and will become traits that you live by. The first trait is that leaders have a vision. They truly practice long-term perspective, and they think from the end. Their decisions are based on what is the next best anticipated step to progress them in the direction of that long-term vision. They are able to avoid many of the ineffective mistakes most people make, because they are always taking planned action based on the big picture. The second trait of leaders is that they take full ownership of doing whatever it takes to realize that vision. They act from a place of "If it is to be, then it is up to me." This doesn't mean that they don't delegate or use leverage to obtain a goal, but they take full responsibility for achieving the desired end result. Third, the leader is a living example of how to be in your power while moving on purpose. The leader is enthusiastic. The leader has integrity. The leader is willing to admit mistakes and to make the corrections as quickly as possible. Leaders govern themselves as if someone were watching their every move, even when no one is. Leaders have the mind-set of whatever it takes, and they back that mentality up with massive action. Leaders constantly build up their teams with love and respect. Leaders have higher standards for themselves than anyone else would ever have for them. Leaders constantly look at how they need to grow in order to lead more effectively to realize the vision. The leader seeks to see the situation from the other person's point of view. In short, as Brian Tracy said, the leader asks questions like "What kind of group would this be if everyone in it were just like me?"

The thing to remember is that you are a natural-born leader. You would not even be reading this book if you weren't. If you can just work a little bit each day to get a little bit stronger with these traits, then over a year's time you will become infinitely greater as a leader. Little by little, these improvements will add up to tremendous growth. It will not always be easy; in fact, at times it will be the hardest thing you could ever do, but you will have a great sense of self, purpose, and accomplishment that no one could ever take away from you.

ACTION STEPS FOR BECOMING A LEADER

1. Choose to be a leader in your life and always act from your vision with the end result in mind.

2. Take full ownership of your vision by realizing that ultimately you are the one responsible for the success of the project.

3. Be a living example of how to conduct yourself for your people by demonstrating the enthusiasm, focus, love, action, and support you want them to display.

#6 Forgive

Forgive. A very powerful action, yet putting it into play can pose quite a challenge. We find it is so easy to hold on to grudges, anger, or any type of unpleasant circumstances that we have been through. Any kind of resentment that you have needs to be released. This is more for your sake than anyone else's. Your judgments about the way you think things should be and how people should act prevent you from being emotionally centered.

The feelings that you hold against yourself or anyone else prevent you from experiencing love and peace in your life. This makes it impossible for you to be free emotionally. Anger is simply stuck energy that has not been released for whatever reason. It is important to understand that holding on to anger is one of the most detrimental things you could do. Clinging to this energy is devastating for your health and wealth. Remember that like attracts like, so anger attracts more negativity into your circle. Anger will actually repel prosperity and wellness and attract even more anger and illness into your life. There is a saying that goes "holding on to anger is like taking a drink of poison and expecting someone else to die from it." This is not to suggest that you will never experience upsets. However, the quicker you let them go, the sooner you will welcome abundance into your life on every level. Carry the loving power of forgiveness with you today and notice how you begin to feel lighter and more at ease.

Action Steps for Forgiveness

1. Forgive yourself and others for all transgressions or unpleasant experiences. This does not mean that you accept all of people's behaviors, but you forgive them for their mistakes and love the God force that exists in them and in all of us, even if some of that force is being blocked at the time.

2. Write out and journal any hurt feelings you may still be carrying. Allow those feelings to come up. If you still are feeling anger you can visualize the other person's perspective and imagine them apologizing to you for the incident. Then gently affirm that you are letting the anger and hurt go. Repeat this process any time the feelings resurface.

3. Do something special to love yourself. Then send love to yourself and the other people you have the feelings toward. Visualize yourself and them doing well in every way.

#7 Guilt

Guilt. Everybody feels this emotion at one point or another. However, some of us feel it more frequently. It usually creeps up when you are disappointed about something you have not accomplished. On occasion, guilt will also show up when you feel that you have violated one of your values in some way. It is very important for your well-being not to dwell on this emotion. When you do, you are usually blaming someone, even if that someone is yourself. You have these feelings when you think there is something you should have done, and then you "should all over yourself." There is a zen proverb that says "should is a stick that we use to beat ourselves with." Blame is always counterproductive. It is a tremendous waste of mental and spiritual energy, and it robs you of the moment.

Everything happens just the way it is supposed to. There are no accidents. However, if you are looking to realize your goals, you must make sure that you extract the lessons that you are supposed to gain from each occurrence or else similar situations will arise with greater impact. The reason for this is because the universe is trying to support your growth so that you can experience more abundance. However, if you are not getting the important lesson then the universe must create an even stronger situation so that you can fully receive the teaching. Therefore, it is imperative to be fully present to the guidance you are receiving from the experience. When you find that you're feeling guilty about something, alert yourself so that you are not dwelling on the past.

Remember that mentally beating up yourself or anyone else will not make you stronger. It will only drain you and hurt your self-esteem. This is quite contrary to what most people think. It is more the norm for people to feel that they have to beat themselves up in order to be able to take action. But this is not coming from a place of love; it is steeped in a mistaken mentality that nothing you do is ever good enough.

A much more powerful way to achieve greatness is to follow the purpose of your higher self. In other words, ask yourself this question: "What is the ideal result that I would like to create with this situation as it is right now?" This way you will be able to meet your high standards and to make whatever adjustments you need along the way. As Wayne Dyer said, "Release yourself from any transgressions you have had today or yesterday." Instead, focus your energy on the present and how you can use what you have learned from the experience to grow.

ACTION STEPS FOR DEALING WITH GUILT

1. Always forgive yourself when you have gotten out of alignment with your ideals.

2. Whenever you feel guilty about anything, notice what personal value of your own you have violated, and specifically figure out what you can do to rectify the situation.

3. Then figure out what you can do in the future to ensure that you are consistently living in alignment with that value from now on.

#8   Selfless Service

Selfless service. When we contemplate our existence, most of the time we evaluate it based on what we have achieved or accomplished in our short time on this planet. Often we rate this by the material things we have accumulated. There is nothing wrong with striving for success or enjoying nice things per se, but measuring your worth by these standards can allow you to get wrapped up in your ego.

We are all unique and gifted, yes, but we are not separate or better than anyone. When you take on the mind-set that all of your actions are to serve God and humanity, which are one in the same, because God is in everything, then you are able to live your life with much greater ease. You can still accomplish and achieve great things, but you are doing it out of a desire to serve instead of a need to be better than others or a need to compensate for any feelings of inadequacy. Zig Ziglar said, "You can have everything in life you want if you'll just help enough other people get what they want." When you are able to reach your goals out of a need to share and serve, you will notice that you no longer have to beat yourself up in order to work hard. This is possible because your work is now being created out of service and no longer to compensate for not being good enough. As this happens you will notice that you are more relaxed. You will be no less intentional or motivated but will work with more flow. You will naturally tap into more of your talents. Even if the work you are doing only involves you, it will still be much more powerful and expressive if it is being done as an offering to God.

All of this goes to say that when you are acting out of your highest self, you are not only more productive and happier, but you will also touch many more people by what you do because of the state that you are in. In short, you will be at peace, and you will be contributing with everything you do. Henceforth, your life's work becomes about much more than just you.

ACTION STEPS FOR SELFLESS SERVICE

1. As you proceed through your day with everything you do, ask yourself, "How may I be of the greatest service both to myself and others?"

2. Link all your activities, like your job, spending time with your family, managing your money, working out, recreation, etc., to your ability to contribute on a higher level. The result will be feelings of increased joy and balance because you will be doing these things from a place of service.

3. Whenever you notice that you are being wrapped up in your ego, shift your focus to contribution.

#9 Power Moves

Power moves. When thinking about reaching your goals, making a shift in your life can sometimes feel like a huge task. Transformation doesn't have to happen all at once. In fact, it rarely does. In most cases it is a process that takes time and consistency in order to establish new habits and create new results. A power move is any kind of action that enables you to establish momentum toward a goal. As Tony Robbins said, "Never leave the sight of a goal without taking some kind of action towards its attainment." Some of these actions can be small, just as long as they create powerful momentum.

Remember *small* is the operative word here. It's not that a power move cannot be big; it can. Massive action is incredibly powerful. However, generally speaking we are much more prone to take action toward something when we have sized it down into baby steps. This makes it much easier for the mind to digest. This is also effective because success normally comes as a result of smaller, systematized step-by-step actions. Also the momentum of the smaller steps can actually lead to massive action because you have built up the muscle of courage and follow through.

In order to make a power move, create a plan with the list of steps you can take to get to where you want to be, and then decisively take the first step. When the first step is complete then take the next one and so on. Initially this may seem pointless, yet this new action will create a snowball effect that will have a tremendous impact with your progress. Even though you will probably have to make adjustments along the way, you will have created a solid foundation to support the process of reaching your objective. Remember the creation of every castle starts with a single brick. By creating a plan and taking powerful action with the next step, you are putting a solid brick in place.

Action Steps for Power Moves

1. Any time you feel in a rut, think of the area of your life that you are dissatisfied with and ask yourself what would you ideally like to have happen in that situation.

2. Then ask yourself why do you want this? Your reasons must be strong enough to make you follow through, even if at times it is hard. Next ask yourself what you can do to make your intention happen, and write out a list of action steps.

3. Prioritize this list of steps. Then decide what is the next most logical and powerful step to take based on where you are now and where you want to be. Then make the power move and take that step.

#10 Planning

Planning. Here's another one, another self-development concept that is constantly overlooked. It is so apparent that many times we cannot see its importance even when it is right in front of us. It is planning. Just as a person cannot run until they have walked, a person cannot excel until they have planned. Steve Chandler says, "Once we get the vision of who we want to be, then definitely planned work is the path to self-motivation. Definitely planned work contains the energy of purpose." In this book you will notice that after you consider many of these principles, it is suggested that you create a list or a plan in order to implement many of them. The reason for this is because planning makes things concrete. It takes something from being a mere concept to something more real that you can mentally grasp. Planning gives you the structure of how you are going to attain what you want and by when. It means scheduling a step-by-step action strategy that can make your vision a reality. Tony Robbins said, "What's talked about is a dream. What's envisioned is exciting. What's planned becomes possible. What's scheduled is real."

Not only does planning come with these significant perks, but it enables you to manage and get the most out of your time. Chandler also notes that every "hour of planning saves you 3 hours of work." While focusing on any goal, remember to come up with a written scheduled plan. Going through this simple procedure will give you a road map to create your vision. It will also have you bypass many challenges that would have otherwise impeded your progress because in fully flushing out the plan, you will anticipate many potential obstacles. Brian Tracy said that "proper prior planning prevents poor performance." Dr. Lee Pulos, the author of *The Power of Visualization*, cites this staggering statistic about planning that says "people who write out their goals with a written plan for their attainment, who constantly visualize and condition themselves, usually accomplish those goals about 99 percent of the time, even if it is not within the time frame that they have originally set up for themselves." As the saying goes, "if you fail to plan, you plan to fail."

ACTION STEPS FOR PLANNING

1. Again with any goal or project you are considering, always ask yourself the question "What exactly do I want?" Be crystal clear and specific.

   Use the Acronym SMART to guide you. S = specific, M = measurable, A = something that requires action, R = realistic (meaning a stretch but doable,) T = timely (meaning when is your deadline going to be.)

2. After you've done this, ask yourself the question "Why do I want this?" Make sure your reasons are emotionally compelling. If the reasons are strong enough you will be unstoppable even when the going gets hard and other distractions come up.

3. Lastly, come up with a specific plan to the best of your ability with the steps you feel you have to take in order to create this. Give deadlines to the steps and schedule them in your calendar. As new steps come up you will schedule them as well, but this will put you into the right kind of action.

#11 Regret

Regret. Not a fun word to be consistently using as part of your daily vocabulary. There is nothing worse than feeling like you have wasted this precious gift called life by not seizing certain opportunities. Do most of us have regrets in our life? Sure, hopefully just a few, and ideally we have used these instances as learning experiences so the same occurrences don't happen again. As the Dai Lai Lama said, "When you lose, don't lose the lesson. Remember that not getting what you want is sometimes a wonderful stroke of luck." There is a way, however, to make sure that for the rest of your time on this planet, you will live without regret.

This way is to come up with a to-do list before you die. As a general guideline, look to write a hundred things on paper to start out with. Be outrageous though; put some big, some small, some in-between things on the list. Don't focus on the how aspect of it to begin with; just get excited and committed about what and why for each listing initially. Make sure it is written down. After you have your list then you can start figuring out how to accomplish it and even enroll people in helping you. Remember, just in writing it down, you are making a commitment, and anytime you fully make a commitment you begin to open unseen doors for yourself.

Afterward type up your list and look at it each day. Doing this is a powerful exercise in that it has you making a decision to never live with regret again. Some of the things on your list may even be going back and correcting some of your past regrets. Also bear in mind that if you have a smaller list of twenty or so and cannot think of any more, you can add on to it later or create a new one after your current list is complete. The size of your list is not as important as the content.

Taking this approach does not mean that you are automatically guaranteed to accomplish every single thing you desire. You may or you may not. However, engaging in this process does mean that you will accomplish far more of them than you would have otherwise. You will be able to have the satisfaction of knowing that you truly went for it, instead of always wondering what could have been. It has been said that most of the things we regret are not what we do as much as what we don't do. This method will have you moving with focus and being very clear about your intentions. Have fun with this, and mark down this day as a turning point in your life.

ACTION STEPS TO AVOID REGRET

1. Write out a list of about one hundred things you wish to accomplish before you die. Type and put the list up where you can see it. Prioritize the list and pick out the top ten goals from it.

2. Create a written plan for these top ten goals with clear deadlines.

   Put up the top ten goals list with the deadlines next to the one hundred things list.

3. Every day look at both lists and follow your plan to achieve your first ten.

   After you have accomplished the first ten, take the next ten from your list and do the same process all over again.

#12　Relax

Relax. Take some time to actually relax. People so often focus on how to accomplish this, that, and the other but don't consider the importance of regenerating. Believe it or not, relaxation actually does help accomplish your goals. It enables you to step back from whatever it is that you are working on and give your mind and body a break. It helps prevent burnout, which so many people experience after starting off strong in an endeavor.

Remember that everything happens best when we are balanced. This is of the utmost importance, because the time away from your project allows you to come back to it with renewed passion and enthusiasm. The time away from your projects also enables you to synthesize and integrate information that you have been processing with anything you have been working on. This is truly a success pattern. Marc Victor Hansen, who is one of the creators of the record-setting *Chicken Soup for the Soul* series, used to take a week of vacation every single month of the year. During this time he would do absolutely no work. As a result of this practice he said that his businesses had never been better. Success really does leave clues.

Another reason that this concept is so important is because if you do not get enough play in your life, then the child within you will basically throw a temper tantrum and sabotage your work. It will be much more of a struggle to get yourself to follow through on what you know you need to do to be successful because you will be so out of balance. Whereas if your inner child gets enough attention, then it will be happy and even support your work.

Now there are two kinds of relaxation, passive and active. Passive relaxation would be an activity like watching television, listening to music, sleeping, or getting a massage. Whereas active relaxation would be more stimulating mentally and physically. Something along the lines of reading, drawing, meditating, playing a sport, or engaging in a hobby could qualify as active relaxation. Both kinds of relaxation are significant but only you can determine which one your spirit needs right now. So today, take a load off. Do something to have fun or pamper yourself and see how it recharges your spirit.

ACTION STEPS FOR RELAXING

1. Schedule your week in advance and make sure that it has a balance of passive and active forms of relaxation.

2. Make sure that you follow through on both forms of relaxation that you have scheduled.

3. With each new week, schedule a variety of different forms of relaxation to look forward to in order to keep this process fresh. Also have at least one day a week where you do no work, only play, relaxation, or both.

#13   Exercise

Exercise. This is a practice that needs to become an intricate part of your daily routine. Health and fitness have an immense effect on your mental and physical well-being. The primary focus of this book is to empower you to realize your dreams and live a life that you love. Exercise is a huge way to do this no matter what your goal is. To begin with, exercise, especially cardiovascular, is not only good for the heart but it also increases oxygen flow to the brain, which enables your thinking to be more clear and sharp.

Secondly, it strengthens your immune system so you are less apt to get sick. The average person has a one in three chance of getting cancer, whereas an athlete has a one in seven chance. You do not have to be an athlete to avoid getting cancer. Simply do something regularly, even if it is walking that gets your blood pumping and the heart working.

Thirdly, exercise will give you tremendous self-esteem and confidence, which are crucial toward any success. Fourth, working out will strengthen your ability to increase the prosperity in your life. There was a study done on the millionaires in this country cited in the book *The Millionaire Mind*, by Thomas J. Stanley that states that over 90 percent of the millionaires in this country work out on a regular basis. Whether or not becoming a millionaire is one of your goals, exercise is a habit of wealthy people that is good to model if you would like to experience more wealth in your life. Fifth, it will strengthen your discipline muscle, which carries over to your other projects. T. Harv Eker has a saying that goes "how you do anything is how you do everything." Discipline will strengthen your productivity in anything you do. Sixth, it will give you increased energy. Finally, it will help you to live longer. The value in this practice is beyond measure because it will greatly enhance your capacity to accomplish your goals. I'm sure you know where I am going with this. So if you haven't already, get an exercise plan and start working it.

ACTION STEPS TO INCORPORATE EXERCISE

1. Come up with a health and fitness goal for the year. Create an exercise plan for this goal and write it out. Put the goal up where you can see it daily.

2. Get some accountability and support for following through on your program, i.e., a coach, a trainer or a friend to work out with.

3. Be consistent and give yourself rewards for every time you complete a workout.

#14 Manifesting

Manifesting. This is the ability to take the concept in your head from being a wish to becoming reality. Here are three major principles to consider with manifesting. This requires some metaphysical understanding, because realizing your dreams is a spiritual process as well as a physical one. As Dr. Wayne Dyer so skillfully pointed out in his book *Manifest Your Destiny*, firstly, "you must realize that whatever it is that you want to attract to you is already in you." This may sound a little odd, so let me put it another way. Your ability to attract what you want stems from a power inside of yourself. So if there is anything in your life that you want but don't have, it simply means you need to use different aspects of yourself spiritually to attract it. In other words, you must tap into your inner resources more deeply so you are in total alignment with what you want. This is where the saying "like attracts like" comes from. You need to feel as if what you are intending is already a reality in your life. The more consistently you hold this feeling, the more you will be a vibrational match with what you want. This match is crucial if you are going to be able to manifest. Most people try to simply take action without paying attention to their vibration. However, as Abraham Hicks said, "No amount of work can make up for a lack of vibration." You must have the vibration first. Again this can be done through meditation, visualization, prayer, and intense focus each day on what you are looking to manifest while feeling like it is already a reality.

Of course it must be very clear that these practices have to be mixed with action in the real world because the inner work by itself is not enough. It will, however, make the outer work easier.

Secondly, "when you are using your spiritual powers to manifest something, keep it to yourself." This process is between you and your spirit, and when you tell others you dissipate the energy, and your ego gets involved. Sharing your spiritual steps with others can often leave you feeling like you need to explain or defend your position. This act takes away focus from the actual process of manifestation and can be very draining.

Third, "have a detached knowing about the whole process." This is another way of saying trust in nature's timetable, knowing that what you desire is already yours; it is just a matter of time before it appears. This reflects Michelangelo's philosophy when he was working on *David*. He said, "The sculpture was already there, I just chipped away at the edges." Use these three keys consistently and sit back and watch the miracles happen.

Action Steps for Manifestation

1. Get crystal clear about what you want. Carry the feeling of your realized intention with you always by spending quiet time with meditation, visualization, prayer, and simply making believe it is already true all throughout your day.

2. As you do your inner and outer work, remember to keep your process to yourself. The only exception to this is if you are working with a coach or someone else to be accountable to with the process itself.

3. No matter what happens along the way while you work toward your goal, be detached from outside circumstances and have total faith in the great outcome in store for you even if it looks a bit different from what you originally envisioned.

#15 Worthiness

Worthiness. This is a critical understanding to have. The saying is true that "if you stand for nothing but the best in your life, most of the time you will get it." All the strategies and techniques in this book can give you access to your best life. However, this access is not enough by itself. Many people will start to apply some of these tools, yet midway through, they will sabotage whatever progress they have made because deep down they have a feeling of unworthiness. This is all too common. When people know what to do but won't fully go for it, the reason is usually because they have a low self-worth. A person may rationalize and say that they felt it was too hard or they didn't have the time or money, but it boils down to feeling like they are not totally deserving of whatever it is that they would like to have in their life.

One thing that is important to bear in mind is that the mere fact that you exist makes you worthy. You are a child of God, and the fact that you have these urges that can manifest in the form of messages, symbols, or signs in your life is God's way of speaking to and through you. So many people mistakenly feel that there is something that they have to do or prove in order to be considered worthy. It is one of the main reasons that some people look to achieve certain goals in their lives in the first place. They feel that after they have accomplished what they are striving for, then they will finally be good enough. The problem with this way of thinking

Is that even if you achieve your goals, nothing you do will ever be enough, because in your mind you were not enough to begin with. This mentality robs you from you experiencing the joy of life and your goals. When you are clear that you are divine because you stem from the divine, then your goals and accomplishments can come from joy and purpose instead of a need to compensate for feelings of being unworthy. Being unworthy is nothing more than a self-created disempowering way of thinking that can be shifted with clear understanding.

So the next time you find that you are selling yourself short, remember that you truly deserve all that you desire. Understanding this emotionally as well as mentally is the first and most crucial step toward manifesting your dreams in a fulfilling way.

ACTION STEPS FOR WORTHINESS

1. Reflect on how it is important to internalize a sense of worthiness so that you are able to be an opening to receive and contribute on a large scale.

    Then remind yourself daily that you are divine by affirming out loud, "I deserve and attract absolutely, positively the best in every area of my life."

2. Pay close attention to your inner urges and any signs, symbols, or messages that come to you about something that you need to do or experience.

3. When you are clear about the guidance that you are receiving from these urges, listen to them without any reservation, and exercise full faith while you follow through on them.

#16 Ego

Ego. We all have it. Some are bigger than others, but all that really matters to you is the size of your own. The ego is not a concept that is often discussed, but its effects can be quite damaging. So what exactly is the ego? Ego has been described as "Earth Guide Only" or "Edging God Out." It is that part of you that keeps you from being in touch with your inner self, your spirit, consciousness, soul, your intuition, or whatever you want to call it. In short, it prevents you from experiencing your God force. The ego is the part of you that disconnects you from your higher power. It makes it impossible to be at peace because it makes you feel unworthy. Ego has you being easily offended, unhappy, and constantly feeling like you are never good enough. Ego has you needing to always prove your worth and how you are better than others.

How can you recognize your ego? When it shows up, it is often judging or rating itself. Frequently the ego will have you comparing yourself to other people. It will whisper in your in ear that someone else is more beautiful, rich, intelligent, accomplished, or smarter than you. Then it will look for some quality that you have above the other person like being craftier, stronger, etc. The ego constantly makes itself feel superior or inferior. It is always weighing and comparing.

Other warning signals of the ego running you is when you easily feel depressed, irritated, cranky, agitated, hyper, or super intense. When you are in touch with your divinity, you are not concerned with differences. You are lighthearted. When you are truly centered, you see the same source manifesting in all people. In this way you are one with the universe and everything around you. In short, you are at peace. Again a secret for getting past the ego is approaching everyone, especially yourself, with unconditional love and respect. This principle is much easier said than done and normally takes a lifetime of practice. So get started today.

ACTION STEPS FOR TAMING THE EGO

1. Notice when you are acting from ego by paying attention to the signs (comparing yourself to others, needing to be right, blaming, justifying, complaining, or making yourself feel bad with low energy feelings like guilt or shame). It also shows up when you need to prove your worthiness or when you cannot see the humor in your current situation.

2. When you have identified ego, shift your focus to your intention, which always comes from love and contribution. Ask yourself in those moments, "What do I want? Why do I want it, and what do I need to do in order to create it?"

3. Practice meditation, visualization, prayer, and affirmations as a way to stay connected to your source naturally and easily release the ego when it comes up.

#17   The Power of Your Word

The power of your word. Do you know the power of your speech? Words carry tremendous energy within them. Certain sounds affect people's states, physiology, and moods more profoundly than others. For example, isn't it interesting how almost all religions use the *ah* sound when referring to their saints or praying. As Wayne Dyer has noted, in Christianity you have *amen*, in Siddha Yoga you have *Rama*, *Krishna*, and *Shiva*. In Islam you have *Allah*, there is *Buddha*, the *Kabbalah*, and *Shalom*. The *ah* sound is prevalent in all of these spiritual pathways because each culture understood the power of words and sound. *Ah* is the universal sound of creation. Another example of the power of your word is if you are a bit frustrated with a situation and you describe yourself by saying you are depressed. This word creates more stress and intensifies the emotion much more than if you were to say you are a little overloaded. It may seem like sugarcoating the emotion, but it literally affects how you feel.

So how does this relate to you? How can you strengthen your word? After all there are countless people in the world that are all talk. They say many things but don't follow through on them. These people have weakened the power of their word. Words not only affect us through sound, but they condition the mind and affect what we attract to ourselves. Remember the phrase "like attracts like." This

Is also true of the words that we speak. You must be mindful about what you say and how you say it.

One of the biggest ways that you can empower your words is by following through on the things you say you are going to do. T. Harv Eker said it beautifully when he stated that "your inner power is the equivalent to the power of your word. No more and no less." This is one of the most crucial principles in this entire book because until this habit is in place then you can never have total trust, happiness, or success. In the same way that you don't trust other people who don't follow through on their commitments, those same feelings transfer to you when you don't follow through on something you said you were going to do.

Keep your promises to yourself and others and only speak in empowering ways. In this way your thoughts, words, and actions are all in sync, and when you say something the universe will mirror your energy and give you much greater support than someone who is just all talk. As a result of this practice you will become a literal magnet for abundance. This may sound a bit metaphysical, and it is, but just begin to experiment with this principle by keeping your word to yourself and everyone else and notice the miracles that begin to show up in your life as a result.

ACTION STEPS TO ACCESS THE POWER OF YOUR WORD

1. Use the science of sound through some form of spirituality to enhance your energy and vibration by meditating, chanting, or praying. The higher your energy, the more success you will attract.

2. Refrain from negative comments and thoughts and only engage in empowering words.

3. Keep your commitments to yourself and others so you build your inner power. This includes commitments to yourself that no one else knows about but you. As T. Harv Eker said, strengthen this muscle by "committing slowly, and completing fully."

#18   Courage

Courage. What does it mean to be courageous? Do you care about how people view you? Are you willing to try something even though you have no guarantees about how it will turn out? Would you be willing to do something even though you might fail and look bad? Are you willing to follow the guidance of your heart even though those whom you are closest to may ridicule you? If you answered yes to these questions, then you have courage. However, for most people, their courage has surges, similar to a wave; it goes up and down.

The way to make sure that you are strengthening your courage is to remember the phrase "to thine own self be true." When you truly listen to your intuition and your heart, your actions will naturally require that you be courageous, because often your agenda will be different from what others think you should do. This can include family and friends.

Another important aspect to understand with courage is that having it does not mean that you will never be scared. In fact because you are listening to your inner voice, it will have you expanding outside of your regular comfort zone, which will initially have you experience fear. This is actually very normal because you will be in your natural state of growth. The key is not to be stopped by your fear. As Susan Jeffers says, "Feel the fear and do it anyway." Eleanor Roosevelt put it another way when she said, "You must do the thing you think you cannot do." The most successful people on the planet get just as scared as everyone else in the world. The difference is that they do not let the fear stop them. They follow the guidance of their highest self no matter what. As the cadet maxim says, "Ask more than others think is safe. Care more than others think is wise. Dream more than others think is practical and expect more than others think is possible." So today, see if you can be silent and listen to your inner voice. Follow its dictates always and you will strengthen your courage. Consequently your life will become the adventurous miracle it was meant to be.

ACTION STEPS FOR EMBRACING COURAGE

1. Become crystal clear about what it is that you want. Go for it 100 percent.

2. As the fear and doubt comes up along the way, realize that it is totally natural and continue to stay in action regardless.

3. Never try to stop your fear because this will only make it worse. Instead acknowledge that it is there, let it be okay and continue to take the necessary steps to accomplish your outcome.

#19 Fun

Fun. Do you have fun? On an average day, do you truly enjoy yourself? Are you known as a fun person to be around? This doesn't mean that you have to do wild, reckless, or outrageous things. It is more about a state of mind. Our moods can be so heavy and significant as we focus on our goals and move through our days. However, if we are not having fun on a daily basis then what is the point of it all. George Bernard Shaw said, "We don't stop playing because we grow old, we grow old because we stop playing." When it comes to achieving our goals we often can get so caught up in the end result that we do not enjoy the process. True achievement is not only accomplishing the desired result but also having fun all along the way. If you are not having fun on a regular basis then it means that you are ignoring a very large part of this equation. A person will never be totally fulfilled unless there is fun in their life.

This can be a difficult balance to strike because we are socialized to think that we cannot play until all the work is done. Yet we must remember that everything happens best in balance, and again if the child within gets no attention, then it will throw a temper tantrum and literally sabotage our hard work. However, the flip side is also true. When you keep the inner child happy by regularly playing and giving it attention, then it will not only let you work hard, but it will actually encourage it. In other words, you will naturally be more motivated.

Fun is not some place you arrive at after you have achieved all your goals; it is something that you carry with you as you take each step of your journey. Sometimes we take ourselves and others so seriously. Lighten up. There is humor in everything if you look for it. Laugh at the world. Be the person whose lightheartedness lifts everyone's spirit, including your own. As you incorporate this new way of being into your life, you will not only experience much more joy but greater overall success as well. So have fun today. Make a habit of having more fun than you would normally allow yourself.

ACTION STEPS FOR HAVING FUN

1. No matter what the activity, make the decision to have fun while you do it. Visualize and affirm yourself having fun with the activity as well as being successful with it. Do this for at least ten minutes total—five minutes of visualization and five minutes of affirmation. Make sure when you visualize and affirm your tasks daily you are at the same time generating a feeling of fun. Feelings are always the fuel for strengthening your inner work and for manifesting.

2. With each task ask yourself the question "How can I make this fun?" By focusing on it with your question, your mind will ultimately come up with answers. Remember to connect rewards to your tasks and activities so you link tremendous pleasure to doing and completing them.

3. Each week, plan and take a fun date with just yourself. Famed author Julia Cameron called this an artist date. It could be something as simple as a movie, a trip to a museum, or even a trip to the bookstore. Just make sure it is planned ahead, done weekly, and done alone.

#20   Karma

Karma. This is a very important principle to be aware of. When we hear this word, we tend to get airy-fairy feelings, but it is a very real concept that is recognized by most cultures and spiritual doctrines. In its most basic essence, *karma* means what goes around, comes around. This terminology is taking the concepts of "like attracts like" and "give what you want to get" a little deeper. Everything you do is an offering to the universe. No matter how big or small, it is an extension of a certain kind of energy that you are emitting. Because we live in a world that revolves around the laws of attraction and vibration, the energy that you send out gets reflected back to you. This is what makes having a clear intention with everything so important. When you are conscious of what you are looking to create, you are much more mindful about what you are doing and how you are being. Most people are unconscious and running on automatic. This is a very limited and dangerous way to live because it creates many unnecessary hardships in your life.

Being aware of the laws of karma means understanding that whatever you do to or for another person will be done to or for you greatly multiplied. This rule also applies to how you treat yourself. Meaning if you love yourself, the universe will reflect that love back to you. The thing about karma is it makes you very conscious of how you act, especially in relationship to others. As Julia Cameron said, "Most people feel more comfortable with the idea that they are not being closely watched." Yet if you honor the principle of karma, you know that even though you can fool people, you cannot fool the universe. This is not something to fear but rather to embrace. If you truly understand it, then you can begin putting good karma in motion for yourself by what you do in the world. So today, with every action you take, be alert to what type of karma you are putting in place. When you are conscious in this way, your next step will always be a perfect one no matter what the situation.

Action Steps for Creating Great Karma

1. Live by the Golden Rule and do onto others as you would have them do onto you.

2. Constantly be growing yourself so that you can use your unique gifts to serve humanity in a wide variety of ways.

3. Deepen your spirituality by meditating, praying, and reading, etc., so that you can have unconditional love for yourself and others while connecting to your source.

#21   Mortality

Mortality. This is probably not a word that you would ordinarily see as inspirational, but it is important to consider. Steve Chandler said, "Most of us like to play the game of life as if our game has no end." We like to feel that there is and always will be a tomorrow. This gives us an indefinite number of times to try and try and try again.

Whereas life may offer many opportunities, we must guard against thinking that we always have another day. This can lead to procrastination. Michael Landon put it best when he said, "Someone should tell us right at the start of our lives that we are dying. Then we might live life to the limit. Every minute of every day. Do it I say. Whatever you want to do, do it now. There are only so many tomorrows." Being conscious of your own death can give your life a greater sense of purpose. Since you don't know exactly how much time you have left and the meter is running, you must give yourself deadlines (no pun intended) for when you will have completed your tasks.

As you think about the end of your life, consider what kind of legacy you want to leave behind. How do you want to be remembered? What would you want someone to say at your eulogy? If you were to make it to be ninety or one hundred years old, what kinds of accomplishments would you like to have had? Norman Cousins said, "The tragedy of life is not in the fact of death, but in what dies inside us while we live." What do you want your life to stand for? In other words, how would you like to leave your mark on the world?

It has been said that "a dream is a simply goal with a deadline." So today, contemplate your own mortality, think about something that is important for you to accomplish before that time comes. When you figure out what it is, develop a game plan. This will help you to honor your time so when the day arrives, you will "not die with your music still in you."

ACTION STEPS FOR EMBRACING YOUR MORTALITY

1. Ask yourself the question "What is the legacy I want to leave?" In other words, how do you want to contribute and serve the world? When you come up with the answer, develop the most detailed plan you can with as many steps as you can think of to get there. Then make the commitment to do it and start taking those steps.

2. Focus on making every single day your own personal masterpiece no matter what you are doing. Constantly ask yourself the question "What would make today an amazing day?"

3. Come up with a To-Do List Before I Die of all the things you want to experience in your life, from travel, hobbies, and material possessions, to great accomplishments and contributions. Then prioritize the list and get busy completing it.

#22 Questions

Questions. Have you ever stopped to think about the power of questions? The potential of human beings is absolutely amazing. It has been said that "we have more potential than we can realize in ten lifetimes." We can accomplish virtually anything if we focus our energy and effort. "Your brain is the greatest computer in the world. It has a storage capacity of about 2 empire state buildings." It has the answer to every question, and if it doesn't have the answer, it knows who to talk to or where and how to look in order to find the answer. The brain will even go so far as to make up answers to some questions if you ask it such ineffective things as "Why do I have such rotten luck or why am I always messing up?" Some other examples of disempowering questions would be "Why does this always happen to me?" or "How come I can't ever get this right?" The answers to questions like these will not only make you feel bad, but they will not support you with arriving at strong solutions to your challenges. Since a big trademark of successful people is that they are great problem solvers, it is ideal to model this trait by being mindful of what you ask so you can ultimately tackle any problem instead of feeling like a victim.

A question directs your focus and "where attention goes, energy flows and results show." Remember the law of attraction. You will always get what you focus on. So if you ask, you will receive. This just means that you must really give your attention to the kind of question that you are asking and expect to get the answer. The quality of your life will be a direct reflection of the kinds of questions that you consistently ask.

For this reason it is very important that we ask our master computer empowering questions. For example, "How can I accomplish this most effectively?" or "What could I do to make this process more enjoyable?" or "How can I accomplish this and have great fun doing it?" As you proceed through your day, practice accessing this surprising power. You will notice not only will you become more productive, but you will also be in a more positive mental and emotional state as well.

ACTION STEPS FOR ASKING POWERFUL QUESTIONS

1. With every challenging situation, always ask yourself, "What is the lesson and the blessing in this situation?" Because everything that happens to you is for your growth.

2. Next ask yourself, "What is my ideal outcome for this situation?" In other words how do I want it to look and why? The reasons why must be strong.

3. Lastly, ask, "What can I do to create that outcome, and how can I do that and have fun at the same time?"

#23 Willpower

Willpower. Another one of those cliché words that all self-help gurus seem to speak of at least once. Your will, your determination to succeed is important of course. Yet it seems so obvious that it doesn't need mentioning, but it does, because you need to understand how to develop it. Willpower comes in different degrees. An incredibly successful person usually has unstoppable willpower. Tommy Lasorda said, "The difference between the impossible and the possible lies in a person's determination." So how does one get to this point? How do you develop a motive so strong that nothing can deter you? The answer lies in your reasons.

You must come up with strong-enough motives as to why you have to do something. What are your reasons why your mission absolutely must be completed, and what will you lose out on if it is not done? In order to have dominant willpower, you need to be connected to your reasons emotionally, even if you have to make the reasons up.

If a person is having trouble following through on a goal of some sort, it simply means that they just do not have strong-enough reasons emotionally to move them to action. Put another way, they just don't want it bad enough. This is absolutely critical to have because even when you are totally aligned with your objective and are crystal clear that it is the right goal for you, there will still be times when you will not be in the mood to take the necessary action. It is in these moments that your reasons will pull you through.

So today think about something that is important, that you would like to accomplish and make sure you have enough strong reasons so that you are disturbed enough to take action and excited enough to pursue your end result. Human beings are motivated by pain and pleasure. Use this understanding to get leverage on yourself in order to follow through when it is hard, because at points it will be. However, it will also be worth it.

ACTION STEPS FOR STRENGTHENING YOUR WILLPOWER

1. Get total clarity about exactly what you want and how you want it to look.

2. Use pain and pleasure to create leverage on yourself and write out at least ten painful ways that it will cost you if you don't realize this goal, and ten ways that it will totally benefit you when you do.

3. If you are still having trouble creating the will to proceed then you either need to create deeper emotional reasons by linking things to your goal that are important to you in life or simply create a new goal altogether.

#24   Resilience

Resilience. Have you ever thought about how failure is crucial for success? Most of the time when we try something and it does not work, we get discouraged. We look at people who we consider successful and we marvel at the way they have accomplished something. How easy it is to forget that these people have had failures too. In fact the most successful people in the world are those who quite often have failed the most.

These people are no different from you. They all have had times when they questioned if it was worth it and if it was even possible. The distinction that sets them apart is their ability to bounce back and keep going. Tony Robbins said, "Surmounting difficulty is the crucible that forms character." The ability to try something new and be flexible in your approach is what makes success happen. Les Brown said that "courage is the ability to go from failure to failure without losing your fire."

For the vast majority of the population, resilience is a weak quality because people look at the mere possibility of failure as more painful than going for something 100 percent. As a result, "the average person will quit something before trying less than one time." Most people take failure personally, as if it were a statement about their worth as a human being. For them, the idea of looking bad is just too great. When in reality, a certain amount of failure is necessary in order for anyone to truly be successful. As Henry Ford said, "Failure is the opportunity to start over again more intelligently." T. Harv Eker said, "Every master was once a disaster." Failure simply enables you to make the much-needed corrections so that you can ultimately have the kind of outcome that you envision. Success is not a linear process. It is more like a wave pattern. Up, down, and all around. The sooner you understand this, the easier it will be for you to be at peace with the process and the quicker you will be able to be achieve what you want. The Adidas sporting good company once had an advertisement that said the following: "Impossible is just a big word thrown around by small men who find it easier to live in the world they've been given than to explore the power they have to change it. Impossible is not a fact. It's an opinion. Impossible is not a declaration. It's a dare. Impossible is potential. Impossible is temporary. Impossible is nothing."

And so it is with you. As you move forward, remember that you are not alone in your struggles to succeed. Millions of people are experiencing these same fears at this very moment. Take advantage of this understanding. As you strive for greatness, reinvent yourself by recommitting to your goals and being flexible in your approach. As a result you will experience each day as being filled with promise. The only way you can really lose is if you give up.

ACTION STEPS TO BE RESILIENT

1. Any time a challenge comes up, always ask yourself three questions: (1) What do I want or what is my outcome? (2) Why do I want it? (3) What is my plan to get it?

2. When a new challenge seems to be really stumping you then come up with a list of twenty ways to handle the challenge that you write down.

3. Make a commitment ahead of time to be flexible and to never give up on your goal (no matter what.)

#25 God

God. To say that this is a huge topic is an understatement. Let's examine your God concept. Don't panic I'm not going to tell you which faith to follow. I'm merely going to give you food for thought in the area of manifesting, which is directly related to your attitudes about God. Being that politics, religion, and money are three of the most charged topics for people to talk about, I am proposing that you simply be open to the possibility of what I am saying.

Most religions or spiritual paths emphasize God (or source or spirit or higher power or whatever you choose to call it) as being both inside and out of everything. However, sometimes we focus more on the outside aspect than the inner. As Wayne Dyer said, "We see God as the great vending machine in the sky and if we tell him how good he is, we believe he will dispense the goodies."

The problem with this overemphasis is that it focuses too much on how we are separate from God and not enough on how we have God in us. When this happens, we do not harness our inner power for manifesting because we think that force is outside and apart from us. Just by realizing that you are connected to God as well as everything else around you means you are acknowledging that what you want to manifest in your life is already in you, because you are one with everything. Hence your ability to attract to you all that you desire in life is a matter of redirecting your internal focus. By consistently contemplating what you want and feeling like you already have it, while taking the steps to get it, you will attract that which you desire in your life or something better. This is a universal law. This process is also much easier if you are clear about your relationship with your source and all that is around you. For some this may be a lot to swallow and may sound a bit airy-fairy, but it works if you truly understand and work it. I suggest that you reread this passage again to let this concept fully sink in.

ACTION STEPS FOR GETTING CLARITY ABOUT GOD

1. Decide to get clear about what God means to you so you can harness your power to attract what you want in your life.

2. Answer the following questions: Is God something I believe in? If so, why? If not, why? If so, how can I deepen my connection with God? What is my relationship with God and all that I want in life? How can I be at peace with myself and other people that have radically different views on this subject matter?

3. Understand that answering these questions will enable you to be in integrity with yourself and be clear about why you believe what you do. These questions will also lead you to ways to deepen your connection with God should you choose to do so.

#26 Treating Yourself and Others

Treating yourself and others. How you treat yourself and others greatly impacts your life. Honoring yourself is the first key. As Julia Cameron said, "You must treat yourself like a precious object because it will make you strong." You must love yourself completely, treating yourself with more gentleness and respect than you could ever expect from anyone else in your world, including family members. The more you do this, the more you will have to give to others, because you cannot give what you do not have.

Many people have an issue with this because they feel they have to beat themselves up so they will work harder and be good enough. This is not coming from love. It is an abusive way of being that will never lead to peace. A person who conducts themselves in this way can never be fulfilled because all of their actions to achieve come from a need to prove that they are good enough. In their mind they think that they will only be worthy or good enough when they have accomplished something great. The problem with this mentality is that it doesn't matter how much you achieve; you will never experience true happiness because the same pattern continues over and over again. There is nothing in the world you can accomplish that will ever have you be good enough. Good enough is not a place that you arrive at. It is a place that you start from. You must have a clear understanding that you are already "good enough." You are divine. You are a child of God. There is nothing to fix.

This does not mean that you cannot have extremely high standards and push yourself to accomplish great things and grow. It simply means understanding that it is much more powerful for your achievements to come from joy and purpose rather than a need to compensate for feelings of being unworthy.

As for how to treat everyone else in your life, Yohon Goerthe summed it up with his quote: "If you treat a person as they are, they will stay as they are, but if you treat someone how they ought to be, then they will become how they could and ought to be."

ACTION STEPS FOR HOW TO TREAT YOURSELF AND OTHERS

1. Determine right now that you are good enough. Be clear that there are areas that you want to grow and expand in, and at the same time, know that you are a divine creation and no accomplishment is going to make you more of a worthy human being. Make the decision that your pursuit of growth is to experience more love, joy, expansion, and contribution, but not to finally be worthy.

2. Whenever you notice yourself slipping into a pattern where you are striving to compensate or be good enough, gently remind yourself that you are already perfect and refocus on your true purpose for pursuing the goal and how it will ideally make a difference in the quality of your life and others.

3. Approach everyone with unconditional love and encourage the best in them. Heed the Dai Lai Lama. "Don't let a little dispute injure a great relationship." This does not mean that you take on other people's challenges or even that you have to spend time with them, but focus on the best in them. (This takes practice because some people will push your buttons more easily than others.)

#27   Living in the Moment

Living in the moment. Undoubtedly, one of the biggest keys to an amazing life is to live according to your own standards. In working toward creating the vision of your dreams you can get so fixated on the results that you don't enjoy the process. You can get so preoccupied with what's next that you don't fully experience the moment, and you can never get that piece of time back. Most people are so focused on the future or the past that they are not able to fully embrace the gift of the current moment. If you were to die today, your next step would not be nearly as important as your experience up to this point. You must learn to be one with the here and now. This is what enables you to get the most out of your present moments.

If your present moments are fulfilling and productive then your life will naturally be great. Each moment is a building block for your future. If each action, thought, and intention is strong, then that moment will be a success. You will still have to learn, grow, and make adjustments, but you will never again feel empty in your current space.

Living in the moment requires that you release any aspects of your past that do not serve you. It means that you are no longer functioning based on your fears and obligations, but instead you are making conscious choice from a place of joy. It means that everything is fresh because all you have is that current segment of time.

So make sure you are present to the experience of each and every second, and enjoy the ups and downs of this ride called life. Because we are never promised another day.

Action Steps for Living in the Moment

1. Look to have a clear intention for each of the anticipated moments of your life by asking these three questions: "What do I want?" "Why do I want it?" and "How am I going to go about it?"

2. Create a mission statement that determines what your "code of conduct" is going to be on a daily basis even for the moments that you can't predict.

3. Practice deep breathing and giving your full undivided attention to each moment of your day so that you are 100 percent engaged in anything that you do.

#28 Anger

Anger. This is certainly an uncomfortable emotion. It tends to be a feeling that we try to stay away from, and understandably so. After all, who wants to have their stomach churning, body tensing, heart racing, and their brow creasing? Yet anger can also be a healthy emotion if it is used properly. Almost like a sixth sense, it alerts you toward something that may not be honoring who you are or who you want to be. Many times this anger, which can also express itself in the forms of jealousy, hurt, or frustration, can point you in the direction of some action that you need to take. It may be a conversation you need to have with someone or a reevaluation of a way that you are not loving yourself. Anger may tell you about a switch you need to make in the company you keep or a new kind of opportunity you need to create in your life.

Anger can also be a great guide for changing your perspective on a particular situation or topic. Since your normal way of being is one of joy, the anger serves as a signal that you are out of balance and that a shift is necessary. Sometimes all that is needed is to look at the situation from another point of view. The phrase "nothing has meaning except for the meaning I give it" speaks to this understanding. This doesn't mean that you don't have challenges, but instead of just glossing over or ignoring them, you understand that the situation overall can only mean what you determine that it means, and since it feels so much better and is a lot more productive to create an empowering meaning, then that is what you do.

Anger is meant to be acted on. Successful people utilize this emotion. They don't run away from it or complain about it being there. As Julia Cameron said, "Anger is not a nice friend, not a gentle friend, but a very, very loyal friend. It will always tell us that it is time to act in our own best interests." So the next time you feel any type of anger, don't avoid it, but instead see what it is trying to tell you. There is a short story that sums up this understanding.

One day an old Cherokee was telling his grandson about a battle that goes on inside of people. He said, "My son, the battle is between two wolves. One is evil. It is anger, envy, sorrow, regret, greed, arrogance, self-pity, guilt, resentment, inferiority, lies, false pride, hate, superiority, and ego. The other is good. It is joy, peace, love, hope, serenity, humility, kindness, benevolence, empathy, generosity, truth, compassion, and faith." The grandson thought about it for a moment and then asked his grandfather, "Which wolf wins?" The old Cherokee simply replied, "The one you feed."

ACTION STEPS FOR DEALING WITH ANGER

1. Any time you notice you are angry, do not try to stop the feeling but instead make a decision to use the emotion and the messages it is giving you.

2. While holding the intention to feel good ask yourself specifically what new perspective or actions you need to take on to correct the situation and honor yourself.

3. Next ask yourself what you need to do or not do in order avoid this situation in the future.

#29 Going the Extra Mile

Going the extra mile. Successful people do the things that failures won't do. They may not enjoy these activities any more or less, but they put aside their feelings regarding the task and they go the extra mile. As Napoleon Hill said, "Going the extra mile puts the law of increasing returns in one's favor." When you go full out, not only are you much more likely to reach your goal, but chances are that you will also surpass it. Are you doing everything in your power to ensure that you get the results you crave? Wayne Dyer said that whenever people have come up to him and said that they visualized and affirmed their goals but they still didn't get what they wanted, he has always asked, "What were you not willing to do in order to get what you wanted?" Going the extra mile simply means doing whatever it takes with no excuses as long as it is legal, moral, and ethical.

The process of going the extra mile also ensures that you tap into a much greater amount of your human potential. The average person only uses about 2 percent of their brain capacity. Even if you were to increase your use to 4 percent, the quality of your life would drastically improve. It is estimated that even the great genius Albert Einstein only used about 10 percent of his brain capacity.

The idea of going the extra mile scares most people because it means constantly stretching outside of your comfort zone. The thing to understand here is that this is simply a matter of habit. Initially it can feel awkward or uncomfortable to intentionally stretch outside of your normal way of doing things, but it is the only way to ensure that you will regularly be in your normal state of growth and reaching new levels of achievement. As T. Harv Eker said, "You have habits of doing and habits of not doing." You want to make the habit of stretching outside of your comfort zone a strong habit. A great way to reinforce this pattern is to do something every day that moves you toward your goals that makes you uncomfortable. If this seems too vague to follow, then simply practice always keeping your word.

Keep your commitments to yourself and others 100 percent of the time. This will constantly have you growing, achieving, and being fulfilled. After a while it will simply be a habit, and it will be more uncomfortable not to stretch yourself than it will be to simply go through the initial discomfort. In other words stretching outside of your comfort zone and keeping your word will end up being your pathway of least resistance.

ACTION STEPS FOR GOING THE EXTRA MILE

1. Continually seek ways to stretch yourself out of your comfort zone and deliver more value to yourself and others than anyone would ever expect from you.

2. With any important thing you are doing, ask yourself "What are five things I could do to over deliver?"

3. After you have the answer to this question, then do either all five things, or at least the three most important things on your list. Make a firm decision to always keep your word to yourself and others.

#30 Creativity

Creativity. In a nutshell it is your gift to yourself and your gift to the world. Since there never has been and never will be another like you in all of time, the more you give your unique expression to things, the more you access and share your gifts. Most people shy away from doing things a bit differently, but remember, your talents are what make the life puzzle complete. Do not forget the people in the world who will not be able to live their mission unless they are benefited by your mission.

On a more immediate scale, creativity is a celebration of spirit coming through you. It makes life enjoyable. When you are not using your creativity, you feel out of sorts. It is like something is stuck inside of you that is yearning to come out but can't. When you block this energy, you can feel antsy, grouchy, and even lethargic. Yet when you release it, your life suddenly has a much greater flow. You are open to receive guidance as to the next perfect way to do something. Ideas and support effortlessly begin to come to you. Your spirit is at peace and you find yourself naturally happy. You are not basing your decisions on what other people are going to think of you but instead on how you can share, express, and serve. In short, you are one with intention.

The other beautiful thing about creativity is that it is one of the quickest and best ways to surmount any obstacle. Remember successful people are tremendous problem solvers. More often than not what is needed to overcome a challenge is simply a little more creativity. For example, if a person is at a loss as to how to get money to start their business because they have no credit and can't get a loan, they may need to consider having a fund-raiser like a bowl-a-thon or partnering up with someone or seeing how they might be able to launch the business using someone else's money or how could they begin with no money at all. Maybe they consider launching the first part of the business online so the overhead is not a factor.

When you practice using your creativity, not only do you get really good at solving problems, but you also start to really enjoy the process. You almost get excited about an obstacle because you see it as a personal challenge to see just how creative you can be. As time goes on you begin to see yourself as unstoppable. Your self-esteem will rise with each situation and your self-concept will grow. As Brian Tracy said, "You can only be as successful as your self-concept." Therefore, increased creativity leads to increased success in all things.

ACTION STEPS TO EMBRACE YOUR CREATIVITY

1. Listen to your intuition with every decision and follow its guidance. This will have you naturally express your creativity.

2. Release the fear of looking bad and reconnect to the understanding that you and the world need your creativity to thrive.

3. Use your creative powers to solve your problems and unleash the joy within.

#31 Legacy

Legacy. Have you ever thought about your legacy? Have you ever really sat down and contemplated where your life has been, where it is now, and where it is going? What do you want your epitaph to say when your time on this planet is up? How do you want to be remembered? What mark do you want to leave on the world? What individual genius do you have in you that is just itching to come out? In order for you to answer these questions you must take time to listen to the voice that dwells within.

Quite often, this inner voice speaks very softly. However, it is imperative that you learn to tune in to it. For if you do, it will lead you to your unique destiny, and you can fulfill your life's purpose. There is a saying that goes "don't die with your music still in you." Most people go to their graves without having even scratched the surface of sharing their gifts. This is one of the great tragedies of life. Not only do you need to express this part of yourself in order for you to be at peace, but also there are actually people in the world who literally will not be able to share their unique gifts if they do not receive yours. In this way the whole world loses out if you don't share the greatness that is in you.

Steven Covey said it best when he exclaimed, "We must take into account the four Ls, which are to Live, to Love, to Learn, and to Leave a legacy." So as you proceed through your day, take time to love yourself by listening to your inner voice, and do something daily to establish your legacy. Keep this Indian proverb close to your heart: "When you were born, you cried and the world rejoiced. Live your life so that when you die, the world cries and you rejoice."

ACTION STEPS FOR LEAVING YOUR LEGACY

1. Answer the question "How do you want to be remembered after you have passed?" Use the four Ls—to Live, Love, Learn, and Leave a legacy to be specific.

2. Write out one hundred goals that you want to achieve in your lifetime that will enable you to measure your greatness and impact on the world.

3. Prioritize your list of goals. Make a written plan for them. Look at the list and work toward your goals daily. When one goal is accomplished, move on to the next one in line. When the list is complete, make a new one.

#32 Unconditional Love

Unconditional love. Love is one thing, but to give it unconditionally to people that you normally wouldn't is an entirely different way of being. We tend to share love with people that we think deserve it because of something they have done or because of our special relationship with them. Yet can you send love to someone simply because we all share the same life force? This is not a touchy-feely love but a feeling of one's connection to everything in the universe.

In order to truly experience inner peace, you must have unconditional love toward all beings and things. Unconditional love sends a message to yourself and others that we are all worthy and deserving of love simply because we exist. There is nothing that anyone has to do in order to be good enough to receive this kind of love. It is simply our birthright because the source that we all stem from is an unconditionally loving source. However, we tend to lose sight of this because we are conditioned to think that we have to earn love like a medal. This conditioning imprisons our spirit in the ego. It makes it so that we are constantly trying to prove that we are good enough and therefore entitled to love. This mentality makes it impossible to be happy because we are always compensating for who we can't be. Hence, we hold other people to the same standard and make our love conditional.

When you give love to yourself and others freely, your life becomes great. You experience joy and peace with much more ease.

Experiment with the feeling of unconditional love toward everyone you see and interact with. See and be with people without any negative judgments or labels. This is can be one of the most difficult things to do. Wayne Dyer says, "The three most challenging things to do in the world are to admit when you are wrong, to defend the person who is absent, and lastly to send love in response to anger or hate." Not only will this help you change your environment, but you will experience bliss as you go through your day. This may be hard at times, but remember that you cannot have love in your life without giving it first—first to yourself, and then others. Satchel Paige said, "Love like you've never been hurt, dance like no one is watching, live as though heaven is on earth."

ACTION STEPS TO EXPERIENCE UNCONDITIONAL LOVE

1. Make the decision that you are worthy of love and do everything you can to demonstrate that love by giving yourself only the best in every area of your life. This includes being kind, loving, gentle, and nurturing with yourself all while having high standards of excellence that you strive for.

2. On a daily basis, visualize and affirm for ten minutes each that you love yourself and are worthy and deserving of the amazing life that you are creating.

3. See how you can pass on love and joy to everyone you encounter, even the people who are edgy or irritable and just watch how you experience more love in your life and how people's attitudes dissolve. This may be as simple as just giving someone a smile.

#33 Success Conditioning

Success conditioning. Success is not something that normally comes easily. The process of succeeding requires stretching outside your normal comfort zone, and usually this is quite challenging at first. At least 80 percent of your success is internal. In other words, the majority of whether or not you will be successful with your goals depends on how you are "mentally, emotionally, and spiritually." You must have the inner capacity to experience the external result that you are envisioning for yourself. This takes a higher level of conditioning than what you have ever had before because your current conditioning has gotten you your current results. Your outer world is always just a reflection of your inner world beliefs and conditioning.

They say every overnight success is years in the making. This is because the amount of time it takes to internally condition ourselves is more significant than most people realize. What percentage of your success would you say is mental? Most people pick a high number, like 90 percent or above. Yet how much time daily does the average person spend on mental conditioning? For most people it is slim to none, and then they wonder why they don't have the life they dream of. The majority of people don't focus enough on this area of success. The average individual will only focus on direct actions. Actions are critical, but a person will not even take all the actions they know they need to take if they don't have the right mind-set. And even if they do take all of them, they won't give them 100 percent of their mind, spirit, and effort if they have a subconscious belief that they are going to fail or if they feel they do not deserve to succeed.

This is why you have to condition yourself mentally and emotionally every day. We are like walking computers. You cannot constantly have good input without having good output. Everything you hear, read, and see affects you. For this reason you must always be studying in your field, as well as studying the principles of self-development. This process is similar to bodybuilding. You cannot just go to the gym and lift weights intensely one time and have the end result of an amazing physique. It takes going to the gym repeatedly on a consistent basis. Even after achieving the desired result, you would still need to regularly go to the gym just to maintain what you have built. Similarly the more you hit the mental gym, the more powerful and successful you will become.

ACTION STEPS FOR SUCCESS CONDITIONING

1. At a minimum visualize and affirm your success at least twenty minutes a day (ten minutes each.) Increase your time to forty or sixty minutes in order to rapidly speed up results.

2. Study in your field as well as in self-development for at least an hour a day.

3. Ask yourself the following questions: "What do I do daily to condition myself?" "Do I use the tools that I have access to?" Ask yourself what you could do to put the odds more in your favor and have fun with the process at the same time. How could you even begin to incorporate the principles that you have read in this book so far? Maybe you could start a hundred and one day program. Perhaps you could work it with a friend in order to have accountability.

4. Whatever answers you come up with, do them.

#34   Motivation

Motivation. This is a juicy concept because we hear it used so much. Yet at the same time, it is a bit of a mystery. Suppose you know exactly what you want and you know precisely what you have to do in order to get it. At this point becoming and staying motivated is the main issue. Most of us already know at least some steps we need to take in order to realize our goals, and if we don't know what to do, we have access to sources that could provide that information. However, as we all have experienced, knowing what to do and actually doing it are two very different things. Quite often it is not even enough to know the strategies and techniques to perform at an optimum level. Such tools as visualization, affirmations, coaching, planning, and writing of goals still require application.

So where do we find this spark, this power, this force called motivation? How do we generate it and sustain it? As cliché as it may sound, the answer lies within you. Victor Hugo said, "The future has several names. For the weak, it is impossible. For the fainthearted, it is unknown. For the thoughtful and valiant, it is ideal." Yet you must fine-tune your ability to get in touch with this power. For this reason, prayer and meditation are absolutely essential. It is through silence and inner focus that you are able to connect with your spirit and summon forth this incredibly powerful force within you that creates spontaneous motivation. Through prayer and meditation you are finally able to do what you know you need to do. Prayer and meditation are huge forms of inner conditioning, and if they are not in place then it can just make the process of doing what you know too difficult to follow through on. So begin, or increase your ability to motivate yourself, by taking time to go within. The more you go within, the more your life will flow.

ACTION STEPS FOR CREATING MOTIVATION

1. Cultivate the habit of doing at least twenty minutes of meditation each day first thing in the morning. Ultimately, add two other twenty-minute segments a day, bringing your total to one hour daily. Or simply do thirty minutes in the morning and thirty minutes in the evening.

2. After meditating in the morning, then use the other power tools of affirmations and visualizations with all your goals for at least another twenty minutes total.

3. Incorporate daily prayer into your morning routine, where you ask the universe and your source to support you with your intentions.

#35 Belief

Belief. Beliefs determine our results, because we end up making them into self-fulfilling prophecies. As Dr. Lee Pulos put it, "first we create our beliefs, and then our beliefs create us." Once a person has a strong belief, they will always act in accordance with it. This process drastically impacts what you look for in your life. As Henry Ford said, "If you think you can you're right, and if you think you can't you're right." Both perspectives are totally made up, yet we make them real. If you believe that it is hard to make a lot of money, then that will end up being your reality because you will only look for vehicles that are hard to make a lot of money with. Remember, "what you think about expands, like attracts like, water seeks its own level." Your beliefs determine your expectations.

For these reasons it is imperative that you identify beliefs that are in conflict with your intentions. If you do not believe that you can do or have something, then even if you have the perfect plan, resources, and support, you will still sabotage your success. This is why it is so important to be able to detect what your predominant beliefs are and where they are taking you. If you want to find out what your predominant beliefs are in any area of your life, simply look at your results.

Asking this question can be a bit of a wake-up call because the answer may be very different from what you would expect. Yet at the same time this information can actually set you free if you use it properly. When you identify the disempowering beliefs that you have that are preventing you from having what you want in your life, ask yourself "What will my life be like several years from now if I carry these negative beliefs with me into the future?" Then create an alternate belief that would support your desired success and begin affirming it daily so that it gets ingrained in your psyche.

At first it may be a little challenging to affirm and live by these new empowering ways of thinking because your mind will not be totally convinced of them. But fully take them on, and live as if they are your new reality. You will begin to notice that you make different choices because of these new files in your mind, and as a result your life will expand. Eventually the new empowering beliefs will gradually replace the old disempowering ones.

Action Steps to Create Beliefs

1. Identify an undesirable result you have in your life. Then ask yourself what belief you have to have in order to experience this result.

2. Next ask what is your desired result in this area? Then ask yourself what new belief would you have to have in order to realize your desired result?

3. Write down five pieces of evidence that support your new belief. For example, if you say, "I am focused and have great follow through," then write down a time when you demonstrated great follow through in your life. Lastly, post your new belief where you can see it regularly and affirm it every day out loud for at least ten minutes.

#36　Baby Steps

Baby steps. Quite often we will not attempt to pursue a goal because it feels like such an overwhelming task. Just the mere thought of taking action is discouraging because of the magnitude of it all. As Tony Robbins said, "The average person tends to get overwhelmed when they think about doing more than three things at a time." Most of the important projects that you avoid taking on in your life will tend to be because they are too big in your head and simply need to be broken down into smaller, more manageable steps. This understanding is imperative because if you stay in an overwhelmed mind-set then you will never get your dream projects started, much less done.

Therefore, do not be afraid of baby steps. If you give yourself the permission to start off slow, then you relieve yourself of the pressure to do it perfectly and having to do it all at once in its entirety. Small progress is much better than no progress at all. Before you know it, you will have created momentum on tasks that at one point simply seemed like too much to handle. As you move forward and take one baby step to move you closer to your goal, you will find that because you have allowed yourself to start off slow, that you naturally end up doing more. Anytime you notice you are not following through on something that you would ideally like to do or have, simply break down the steps to the point where mentally you feel they are very doable and still productive.

Remember, always make it easy for you to win.

Action Steps for Taking Baby Steps

1. Get crystal clear about what you want. In other words, determine what your specific measurable goal is and write it down.

2. Determine what the major steps are that you will need to take in order to achieve the goal. Write the steps down and prioritize, date, and schedule them.

3. For each of the prioritized steps, break them down into smaller steps so the project becomes manageable. For example if the goal is to write a one-hundred-page book, then a smaller more manageable step may be to write every day for at least twenty minutes.

#37   Laughter

Laughter. Laughter has tremendous healing power. People who laugh a lot tend to have lower blood pressure, be less stressed, and live longer. Laughter has even been known to cure cancer in some cases. When you laugh, endorphins are released in the brain. These endorphins create a natural high that is good for the body and the spirit. Human beings are the only animals that have been endowed with this gift. When you are able to laugh at your situations, you lighten your loads by creating more ease. Not only does it lighten your burdens, but it also improves digestion and reduces all things to their proper size.

When you can laugh at yourself, it is a great sign that you are centered. When you are connected to your source, you tend to naturally be lighthearted and more playful. If you cannot see the humor in your current situation then you are probably stuck in your ego. This blocks energy and makes success in life much harder and less fun. As Og Mandino said, "Man is most comical when he takes himself too seriously. Therefore, be able to laugh at your failures as well as your success, and never allow yourself to become so important, so wise, so dignified, and so powerful, that you forget how to laugh at yourself and the world."

Practice cultivating the habit of laughter. Watch movies that crack you up. Spend time with people who are lighthearted. If a person is not able to laugh then they can only be but so happy. And without these two elements of happiness and laughter, one can never be a true success in life, no matter what they have accomplished.

ACTION STEPS FOR CREATING LAUGHTER

1. Make a decision to be a lighthearted person.

2. On a daily basis look for the humor in your various situations and remember that you are closest to your source when you are experiencing a lightness of being.

3. Watch funny movies and spend time with funny friends and family regularly.

#38   Keeping Good
Company

Keeping good company. It has been said many ways. "Only quality people. If you want to fly with the eagles you can't swim with the ducks." "Who you spend time with determines your destiny." Whatever catch phrase you use, the sentiment is always the same, in that the people in your immediate circle of influence have a tremendous impact on your life. Brian Tracy says "99 percent of your success is directly related to your reference group." When you consistently surround yourself with a group of people, they affect you whether you want them to or not. If they are positive, then their positive mind-set and vibrations will rub off on you. If they are negative and tend to have a lot of baggage or other issues, then these are more forces that you have to guard against, even if you have high energy.

In order to fully grasp this concept, recall a time you spent with someone and afterward you were totally drained emotionally or physically. Now think of another time when you were in the presence of someone and afterward you felt a certain lightness of the heart. Your motivation, enthusiasm, and overall zest for life were higher just because you were in their presence. Each situation had the opposite effect because of who you were surrounded by. There is a saying that is applicable here that says, "Environment is stronger than willpower."

It is important to identify who these energy leeches are. All human beings carry energy. Some are high and some are low. We must be particularly cautious about being around the low-energy individuals. The effect of these people can be so detrimental that you can have clear goals, specific written plans to achieve them, and even learn the greatest techniques of achievement, but if you are constantly spending time with people who have low energy and aspirations, then this alone can be enough to sabotage your success.

Often times these low-energy people may be friends or family members. This does not mean that you love them any less; it is merely a signal that you must be mindful about whom you spend large amounts of time with and more importantly with whom you share your dreams. It is difficult enough to realize your goals in the world at large. Avoid compounding this challenge by making your inner circle another force to overcome.

Action Steps for Keeping Good Company

1. Take a sheet of paper and draw a circle on it.

2. Think about three people that make you feel empowered with your ambitions, and write their names on the inside of the circle. Then think of three people that you have to guard against when you need to be at your best, and write their names on the outside of the circle. Just by having this awareness, you will make it easier for you to keep your energy strong.

3. Make a decision to spend less or no time at all with the people outside the circle and more time with the people in it.

#39 Time

Time. Besides your health, it is the most valuable thing you have. It is mysterious and mischievous. You cannot see it, taste it, or touch it. Yet despite being intangible, it surely exists. The value of your time is difficult to put in words. It has quite often been said that it is the greatest gift that you could give to someone. However, cherishing it is also one of the greatest gifts you can give to yourself, because there is absolutely no way to get it back. Once a moment is gone, even if you are fortunate enough to have a new one, there will never be another moment just like that one ever again.

When your time on this planet is up, all the money in the world cannot buy you another day. The other thing about time is that the older you get, the faster it seems to go. Can you believe the number of years you have already spent on this earth? You need every ounce of time in order to accomplish anything worthwhile.

When you look at any regrets that you may have in life, the vast majority will be related to a lack of planning, thinking ahead, and ultimately getting more out of your time. Many missed opportunities occur simply because a person does not have longtime perspective and is not clear about what their priorities are. Truly successful people think long term, are clear about their values, and act accordingly.

Whether you are responding to some immediate situation or working on a project, it is crucial to understand that only 20 percent of your actions are going to get you where you want to be. In other words, If you have a list of ten things to do, only about two of those things are really going to have a significant impact on you realizing your specific goals. This is called the Pareto principle or the 80/20 rule. Most people spend the bulk of their time on the other 80 percent of things to do and wonder why they are so unfulfilled in life. Therefore, in order to truly honor your time, you must focus on the important 20 percent tasks at least 50 percent of the time. You will begin to notice that as you respect this principle, you will get more out of life, and time will begin to be your friend. Even when you don't get everything done you will still be much more fulfilled. As a result, your energy, success, and self-esteem will skyrocket.

ACTION STEPS TO HONOR TIME

1. Get crystal clear about your goals both short term and long term and write them down.

2. Come up with a specific written plan and the steps needed to accomplish your goals. Then prioritize the goals and the steps in order of importance.

3. Schedule and follow your daily plan, and avoid getting interrupted and sucked into urgent and unimportant tasks by constantly asking the question "Is this activity part of my 20 percent?" Only do lesser tasks after you have completed the 20 percent ones.

#40 Money Beliefs, Part 1

Money. What was your response when you read this word? Did it bring up baggage for you? Did your mouth water? Did your lip quiver? Did your brow furrow? Did you suck your teeth? Did you put on a big smile? Most people have mixed associations when it comes to the almighty dollar. Sure they would love to have a ton of it, yet there are many other less optimistic feelings they have as well, such as "money is the root of all evil." "People who have money are selfish or inconsiderate." Or "if you have a lot of money people will try to take it all away from you." Or "in order to get a lot of money you would have to work so hard that it's not even worth it." "Money does not grow on trees." "Only super talented people have money." If a person really dissects all of these mixed associations about money, it is easy to see why they may not have the level of abundance they deserve.

Someone reading this may think that the reason they are not where they want to be financially is because they had a bad business partner or the economy was down or because they simply just had a bad break of some sort. However, the thing to remember is that same person attracted those exact situations into their life in the way that they affected their financial success. Remember 80 percent of your success depends on how you are mentally, emotionally, and spiritually. Money is no exception to this rule. As T. Harv Eker said, "We all have a financial blueprint that is set for a specific level of success with money, and this blueprint will tend to stay with us for the rest of our lives unless we identify it and intentionally change it."

The first step in creating prosperity is to simply acknowledge what the disempowering beliefs are that make up your financial blueprint. Again, in order to determine what your predominant beliefs are about money and abundance, simply look at your results. This is the best way to see what kind of financial success you are really programmed for. Many of these beliefs stem from childhood, either from parents, certain experiences you may have had, or from things you consistently heard growing up. If you don't have the level of wealth in your life that you want, then you have some of these negative attitudes about abundance. As Tony Robbins said, "If you don't have enough money, there is only one reason. You associate more pain to having it then to not having it, because surely you are capable of generating it."

ACTION STEPS FOR DISCOVERING AND CREATING STRONG MONEY BELIEFS

1. Describe an undesirable result in your current financial life. Write out what belief you had to have in order to experience this result.

2. Describe your desired financial result in this area. Next, write out what new belief you would have to have in order to realize your desired result.

3. Write out five examples in your life that can serve as evidence to support the new beliefs. Affirm the new belief every day for at least ten minutes with tremendous enthusiasm.

#41 Prosperity/ Money, Part 2

Prosperity. Once you have examined your attitudes about money and have gotten clear that you are going to shape them in order to have the level of wealth you deserve, there are three things that you must keep in mind. First, in the immortal words of Marsha Sinetar, "do what you love and the money will follow." The only way to experience mastery, Wayne Dyer said, "is to truly enjoy what you do." When you master something, you increase your value to the market place which promotes wealth. (An aside, 74 percent of wealthy people are entrepreneurs.) Second, be frugal. As Thomas J. Stanley, the author of *The Millionaire Next Door* put it, the number one characteristic of millionaires is frugality. Put another way by T. Harv Eker, "rich people are excellent money managers. It doesn't just matter how much you have, but also how well manage what you have." Even if you are in debt, once you show the universe that you can handle what you already have, then you will be rewarded with more. Keep track of all you spend. Always pay yourself first. Have a money management system. Spend less than you make and invest in a disciplined fashion to create passive income. Treat money like a living entity. When you honor and take care of it, it will honor and take care of you.

Most millionaires spend twenty hours a month on financial planning. Third, design an actual plan. Have this plan cover both the offensive and the defensive aspects of wealth accumulation. Offensive in that you do something you love in order to make money, and defensively in that you spend beneath your means and have your money make money for you. This is true of investing because it creates passive income. "A person can never be totally free unless they have enough passive income to pay for their desired lifestyle," T. Harv Eker said.

This means that you have set up vehicles that bring in money for you on a regular basis without you having to work for it. Ideally you will do this in such a way that you have multiple streams of passive income. This would mean stocks, real estate, businesses, or some form of "infopreneuring," such as writing a book and receiving residual payments on it. Lastly your plan must be backed up with purpose and action. This is a lot to digest, but money is such an important area of life that most people fail in. Therefore, you need to give it specific attention. I would suggest reading this section over at least thirty times so that the concepts become ingrained in your consciousness.

ACTION STEPS FOR CREATING PROSPERITY

1. Figure out a way to do what you love so that it provides massive value for people and can create great wealth for you.

2. Honor your money. (1) Tithe 10 percent of everything you make. (2) Constantly increase your income. (3) Ultimately invest at least 10 percent of it. (4) Save at least 10 percent of all you earn. (5) Simplify your lifestyle by spending less than you make. (6) Create multiple streams of passive income to be financially free. Read T. Harv Eker's book *Secrets of the Millionaire Mind* and adopt his Jar money management system.

3. Have a clear written financial plan that covers the six main aspects of wealth mentioned in step two. Be especially focused on creating passive income streams.

#42   Patience

Patience. How much do you have? For most people the answer to this question is far less than they need in order to have ease with their success. We are the instant microwave generation. We want everything and we wanted it yesterday. We also want each thing to go exactly how we would like, with everyone acting how we think they should. In having this attitude, we are not allowing ourselves to move along with nature's flow.

The great creator has its own time table, and most of it is not instant. The majority of nature's greatest miracles take time. The Chinese bamboo tree requires consistent watering every single day for six years, and at the end of that period, within a matter of weeks, it grows to be around ninety feet tall. Yet patience and consistency are required, for if one day of watering is missed, its growth will be stunted. And so it is with you.

It has been said that "success is a zigzag, not a straight line. In fact there is no such thing as a straight line in the entire universe. Even the straightest line will have a slight bend and curvature to it when it is looked at under a microscope." Your pathway to success is the same exact way. It is very much like a swerving road as opposed to a straight shot. This is a very important understanding to have because most people think it is a straight line in which they just determine what they want, create a plan, follow it, and then they will have the expected result. However, the reality is that quite often you will constantly have to make adjustments because a lot of what you do in the beginning will not work. You can cut down on some of this time by modeling people who have already accomplished what you desire, but even with this there will still be a learning curve. If you do not have this understanding then when the road blocks appear you will not have the emotional stamina to withstand them and you will give up.

Success requires tremendous patience. Your journey will require action, feedback from your action, and then adjustments based on that feedback. In other words, you will have to constantly "correct and continue," as T. Harv Eker said.

Sure have goals, sure have deadlines, sure have a plan, but also have the wisdom to know that everything great takes time, and often more than we would like. Swami Muktanda said, "Remember God loves you and fulfill all of your needs. He will give you everything when the time is right." So be patient and prepare yourself to have what you want and when the time comes, you will be ready to receive it.

ACTION STEPS FOR PATIENCE

1. Declare at the beginning of any important project to *never* give up.

2. As challenges surface, simply "correct them and continue."

3. When something you do does not work, remind yourself that you are one step closer to your goal, and model other successful people who have what you want.

#43 Balance

Balance. Everything happens best in balance. When you look at the four main quadrants of your life, it is apparent how this works. For example, it is easier to honor your body if there is harmony in your relationships, and it is easier to give energy to your dream project if you are in integrity with your money. At any given time one of these areas may require more attention than the others, but this is the very nature of creating balance. This process is a constant juggling act that takes practice in order to master it. To really grasp this concept, think of a high-performance sports car like a Porsche. Even though this machine has incredible power and speed, if one of the four wheels is not balanced then the ride is going to be much slower and not nearly as smooth. However, when all the wheels are in perfect alignment, this machine then becomes one of the greatest performance vehicles in the world.

In order for you to perform at the highest level, you must constantly evaluate what needs to get attention in order to maintain balance in your life. This involves prioritizing as well as consistently doing important activities in each of the four quadrants. You must regularly take significant action to further your health and fitness, finances, relationships, and dream projects.

Maintaining balance also requires sensitivity to what needs attention. If you have been working really hard, your spirit may require some downtime or a really fun activity that you don't normally allow yourself to do. If you have been playing a lot, you may need to give some attention to your finances and your future wealth. You may need to plan some quality time with your family, friends, or both. Even with reading this book, it is important to ask where you are right now. How much of this information have you implemented into your daily routine? Let's take the best-case scenario and say that you have applied most of the principles in some way or another. It is still important from time to time to take a personal inventory and assess yourself and see what needs attention. What tool or principle would make the biggest difference in your life if applied right now? Whatever it is, use today to create balance, and you will find that you will be much more happy and successful.

ACTION STEPS FOR BALANCE

1. Have long- and short-term goals that you set in each of the four quadrants of health and fitness, finances, relationships, and your dream projects and have a written plan for each.

2. Take regular steps each week in all four quadrants in order to maintain balance and avoid many problems that would otherwise come up.

3. Each day and week, ask yourself what needs to be done in order to maintain balance and create the highest quality of overall life for you. What area of your life do you feel is lacking and needs attention the most? When you have the answer, take immediate action.

#44   Risk

Risk. When we hear this, word we tend to think of danger. Avoid it at all costs. Proceed with extreme caution. Yet a risk can be one of the healthiest, most empowering things for you to take. Shakti Gawain said, "The universe will reward you for taking risks on its behalf." The scary thing about risk is that it propels you into the unknown. You may find it so much more safe and familiar to remain in your normal comfort zone, where you know how everything works and how everything is going to turn out. The problem is that it costs you to remain in this place. Even though it may feel very secure, it prevents you from growing.

To put it bluntly, our lives feel empty and meaningless if we are not growing. Think about it for a second. The times that you are most proud of in your life tend to be times when you took on a challenge and performed exceptionally well, or you found yourself in a new and scary situation and rose to the occasion. Another time may have been when you simply had a vision and had the courage to go after it. All of these scenarios came with some kind of risk. You cannot accomplish great things and truly be alive if you do not take some risks. It is the only way to grow. As Les Brown said, "if we are not growing and moving towards our goals and dreams, we are committing spiritual suicide."

Success requires risk, risk of looking bad, risk of failure, and risk of experiencing challenges. This is part of the price that must be paid in order to have all of the tremendous rewards that come from realizing your dreams. Yet this price is well worth it. This does not mean you should act foolishly but instead to take calculated risks and to constantly expand outside of your comfort zone. It takes constant practice to make this muscle strong, but after a while it will be part of your normal way of being, and as a result, success will become your pathway of least resistance.

Action Steps for Taking Risks

1. Calculate the risks that are required to realize your intended outcome, and take the smartest ones even though they make you uncomfortable.

2. Visualize yourself successfully taking these risks and feeling great about the results every day until they are accomplished.

3. Practice regularly doing things that stretch you as a person even when they are not necessarily linked to a specific goal of yours. Take a risk today that would have your world expand, even if it is in a small way.

#45 Flexibility

Flexibility. Have you ever had something that you really wanted to do or have, but no matter how hard you pushed, you simply were not able to get it? This means you need to change your approach. It has been said that "lunacy is doing the same thing over and over again, the same exact way while expecting a new result." As the saying goes, "if you always do what you have always done, then you'll always get what you have always gotten."

Success in any calling not only requires persistence but an ability to analyze your situation and to see if your strategy is working or not. If it isn't, then flexibility is the key. If a person is not willing to be flexible then they are losing precious time. Many people fail because they are simply stuck in one way of doing something. Gail Sheehy said, "If we don't change, we don't grow. If we don't grow, we aren't really living." Being rigid can stem from the need to be right or fear of exploring the unknown. Whatever the reason, the cost is too great.

It bears repeating that success is a zigzag and not a straight line. If you are fixated on succeeding in one particular way then you are ignoring the zigzag. If a person cannot bend when a plan does not work, then as the pressure increases they will break. This concept is similar to certain martial arts forms. Various styles train you to take the force of your opponent's blow and to literally use their own momentum and energy against them. The term "go with the flow" does not mean to be complacent but rather to pay attention to the feedback you are getting from your efforts, constantly make adjustments, and continue to move forward with clarity about your intention. Your plan may be perfect, but the majority of the time it will require some adjustments even if they are slight. For this reason, flexibility is imperative to success. If you do something that doesn't work, simply do it another way. Eventually you will strike gold.

ACTION STEPS FOR FLEXIBILITY

1. Make a firm decision before any important project to be persistent, and understand that it is normal to experience challenges especially in the beginning.

2. Take something you have been struggling with and come up with a totally different game plan. Then work the new plan.

3. Create a lifelong habit of quickly facing challenges and immediately asking what is next and how else might you go about it.

#46 Generating a Peak State

Generating a peak state. This is a term that has been frequently used by Tony Robbins. When the principles and techniques in this book are applied, they can create astonishing success. However, in order to do this at the highest level, you must be in a peak state. In other words you must be in the right frame of mind and have the proper focus, energy, and enthusiasm with whatever you are doing. If these things are not in place then you are starting at a disadvantage. One of the trademarks of successful people is that they are masters at putting themselves in a peak state. This means that they are able to get in the zone and create these high levels of focus, energy, and enthusiasm even when they are not in the mood. The only way you can do this is if you know how to shift your energy and generate a peak mental and emotional state. What do you do to feel your absolute best? What makes you feel powerful, alert, and full of energy?

Some of the best ways to achieve this are getting a great night's rest, eating a very healthy meal, listening to some of your favorite music, working out, and even wearing certain outfits. Each of these examples is a great place to start. As far as sleep is concerned, sometimes getting as much as nine or ten hours rest, if possible, is the absolute best thing you could ever do because the result will be that you wake up supercharged and full of energy. Eating well is also great for creating a peak state because if you eat enough foods that alkalize your system like raw greens, your energy will dramatically rise. Because of this, you will not require as much mental willpower to get things done. Music is one of the greatest state producers of all time. Just think about how you feel when you listen to one of your favorite songs. You just naturally want to move more, whether it is dancing or simply being more active. As the saying goes, "motion creates emotion." Use music to pump yourself up and walk, talk, and move with the attitude of success.

A great thing to mix the music with is working out. Because you will already want to move, the exercise process will be much easier to start and more fun to do. Once you begin, the energy of the process will usually just carry you all the way through the workout session. Working out by itself is great because it makes you feel more aggressive about pursuing your goals, but combined with music it doubles your effectiveness. Exercise also has you feel better about your body and raises your self-esteem overall. There is a saying that goes "you can't do well unless you feel well." Clothing is another great tool for generating a peak state. Think of a time that you just knew you looked like a million bucks. You naturally had more energy, enthusiasm, happiness, and zest for life at that moment. This feeling is available to you at all times. When you need to have peak energy simply take out one of your favorite feel-good outfits and wear it. You will instantly begin to feel more confident and entitled to the success you crave. It is important to know how to push your own buttons in order to trigger empowering emotions. The better you feel about yourself, the easier it is to be motivated.

ACTION STEPS FOR GENERATING A PEAK STATE

1. Make a decision each day to practice putting yourself in a peak state by doing something that moves you toward your goals even when you are not in the mood.

2. Experiment with the examples above and decide which tools work best for you.

3. Pick out at least three great options for you to use with music, clothing, healthy foods and ways to work out to quickly help you generate a peak state.

#47   Clutter Clearing

Clutter clearing. In feng shui, which is the Chinese art of placement, clutter is considered "the number one cause for a lack of success in any calling," exclaims Alex Stark, who is one of the world's greatest feng shui masters. That means if a person is not getting the results that they want in the realm of money, relationships, business, or health, in some way it can be traced back to clutter that they have in their life. The reason for this is because the person has a subconscious belief that the universe will not supply them with whatever it is they want and as a result there is a holding on. You cannot attract anything in your life that you are not a vibrational match with. Most people that have a significant amount of clutter in their lives have experienced a significant loss at one point or another.

Clearing clutter is one of the greatest ways to move stuck energy and put you in alignment to attract what you desire. Clutter is anything you do not love, use, or that does not honor who you are. If a person has excess clothes that are never worn, unpaid bills that are piling up, stacks of papers, magazines, or any other things that they no longer need or use, then they are adding clutter to their life. Clutter clogs up the pathways of abundance mentally, physically, spiritually, and financially. For example if you go in your closet and there is a piece of clothing that you haven't worn in a year and half and it has no real sentimental value, then get rid of it. Give it to the Salvation Army, the Goodwill, or someone who you know can get good use out of it. Clutter clearing is also a fantastic way to get organized with your work. Clutter cannot exist when one is truly organized. If you go into your drawers and your papers are all scattered, organize them and throw out any you no longer need. Look to maintain this clear, clean state because if it is difficult for you to get in, through, and around your home or office, then it is difficult for the abundant energy to get in your space as well. Your relationship to your space reflects your relationship to the world.

Take on the mind-set that less is more. When you simplify your life, you will be more at peace. The other amazing thing about clutter is when you get rid of it, wonderful new things come into your life. This principle also holds true for relationships. Clutter can also include people. Remember you want to spend the bulk of your time with people who are going to lift up your energy. Do not fear releasing toxic people from your life, because as you do, other like-minded people will come into your circle to fill the void. In fact the only way you can attract quality people into your life is to release those who are draining your energy. The release is what is necessary in order to create the space for this to occur. Many people fear releasing clutter because they feel that if they only keep things that they love, use, and honor who they are then they will not have much of anything left in their life. This is having a scarcity mentality that creates more scarcity. You must remember that the release is what creates the opening for you to receive.

Declare that you have the intention to have only the best in every area of your life. The universe always mirrors back to you the energy and the intention that you are sending out. For this reason as you clear clutter out of your life, it is worthwhile to say the affirmation "I have absolutely, positively the best in every area of my life." This way as you release what no longer serves you, it will be replaced by only the best, the best in the form of opportunities, people, wealth, and health. When you are getting rid of clutter, you are doing well with what you have, and as the saying goes, "those who do well with what they have will be given more."

When you have this intention and only keep things that you honor, love, and support who you are, then you become a magnet for abundance on all levels. I have had clients honor this principle by cleaning out their homes and offices, and within a month, week, even a day at times, have gotten new jobs, promotions, raises, and have literally even found money. One client of mine was cleaning out his office and basically found three thousand dollars. He had done an arbitration case two-plus years ago that he had never collected on. He found the statement, sent in the invoice, and ended up getting the money shortly afterward. The reason this happened is because he was honoring that universal law that says those who do well with what they have will be given more. This is why the rich get richer. The universe sees that you can handle what you already have. Therefore, in the beginning when you are clearing clutter it may feel like you are just getting rid of everything, but ultimately what will replace it will be "only the best."

ACTION STEPS FOR CLEARING CLUTTER

1. Make a daily habit of at least fifteen minutes of clutter clearing per day.

2. Immediately release anything that you don't love, use, or that does not honor who you are.

3. Spend your time with quality people and affirm daily that you have "only the best" in every area of your life.

4. Have your home feng shuied by someone who is a master.

#48 Faith

Faith. What would you attempt to do if you knew you could accomplish it? The dictionary defines faith as "belief that does not rest on logical proof or material evidence." Faith can be a difficult thing to have because it is total trust in the universe's ability to support you in manifesting your dreams. To begin with, you must release any feelings of unworthiness and understand that you are worthy of all the abundance the universe has to offer because you are a part of it. In other words, abundance is your birthright. Eileen Caddy said, "Expect your every need to be met, expect the answer to every problem, expect abundance on every level." You may feel like you are not totally worthy because of what someone has told you or because of failures that you have had in the past, but this perspective is just a made-up interpretation that is creating unnecessary blocks in your life. Susan Jeffers said, "We have been taught to believe that negative equals realistic and positive equals unrealistic." The great creator brings us messages in many ways. One of the main ways is by speaking to us through the small voice that comes from inside that we label as our intuition. Part of getting over the hump and realizing the life of your dreams is simply understanding that the very fact that you have an inner urge to do something in the first place is the spirit's way of signaling you to take action. There is a saying that goes "what you want wants you even more."

Having faith can also feel scary or challenging because it is like jumping into the unknown. But this is where the juice of life is. If people had to know all the answers to something before they realized an intention, then no one would ever accomplish anything. It is an integral part of your success for you to exercise this muscle called faith. Apply your faith from the very beginning of any pursuit in order to move past the fear of the unknown or any feelings of unworthiness and to begin to tap into your vast potential.

Faith boils down to trust—trust in yourself, trust in your vision, and trust in the universe. The most successful people on the planet have the ability to listen to and trust that inner guidance even when their vision may have looked impossible to achieve. Claudia Black said, "Trust in yourself. Your perceptions are far more accurate than you are willing to believe." Therefore, model this pattern of success even though it will be scary at times and you may often have doubts and want to quit. Henry Thoreau said it best when he summed up living in faith by saying, "If you go confidently in the direction of your dreams and dare to live the life that you have endeavored, then you will meet with a success that is unexpected in common hours."

ACTION STEPS FOR EXERCISING FAITH

1. Make a promise to yourself to listen to your intuition and to have faith in your visions no matter how many times you fail.

2. Always expect the best in life and remind yourself of your entitlement to these blessings daily so it is easier to exercise faith with beginning, continuing, and finishing any goal.

3. Use the power tools of meditation, journaling, affirmation, and visualization to stay connected to your vision and to strengthen your faith.

#49 Patience, Part 2

Patience, part 2. This word can be tricky because you don't want to use it as a form of procrastination. It is very easy to not do all you can to produce certain results and to call it being patient. However, once you have gotten past this point and you are at the stage where you are putting forth the necessary effort, you may tend to want results immediately. Patience is required in order to create any great work. As Og Mandino, the author of *The Greatest Salesman in the World*, said, "nature acts never in haste. To create the olive, king of all trees, a hundred years is required, whereas an onion plant is old in nine weeks. I have lived as an onion plant, it has not pleased me." Patience requires a certain amount of letting go of your control. Again, trust is needed in order to be fully patient. A person who has total trust in themselves and their creator can have what Dr. Wayne Dyer called detached patience. In other words, if your dream does not crystallize exactly when you want it to, you do not fret because you have an inner knowing. You fully understand that you will indeed have your dream or something better when the time is right. The fact that your dream hasn't happened when you predicted just serves as a reminder to you to continue to prepare for it so you are equipped to receive it.

With patience, you still do the necessary work, but you trust that nature has its own timetable and that you will achieve your results when the great creator says it is time. This applies to business, money and everything else. Shakti Gawain said, "The more we learn to operate in the world based on trust in our intuition, the stronger our channel will be and the more money we will have." Again the one thing you can do to speed up your productivity is to role model. Find someone who has what you want and learn from their success. Do what they did that worked and avoid their mistakes. If they can do it, so can you. As Will Smith said, "We're all pretty much created equal coming out of the womb, some of us just get more out of ourselves than others." So role model someone today, while at the same time having patience with the universe's schedule. It is all about balance.

Action Steps for Creating Patience

1. Determine before any project to put forth the necessary effort in order to have the end result so that you can feel confident that you are doing your part.

2. Whenever you do not meet one of your timelines for accomplishing a goal, simply set a new date and make the necessary adjustments.

3. Search out, study, and role model people who have what you want, and remind yourself any time you get frustrated or impatient that nature has its own rhythm and you will get everything when you are ready. Always remember that your job is to simply trust and continue to prepare by growing yourself.

#50   Decision Making

Decision making. What makes people successful? There are many factors, some more obvious than others. Some of the more popular ones are hard work, perseverance, and faith. However, one of the areas that many people underestimate is the importance of decision making. To make a decision means to cut off from any other option. As Tony Robbins said, "Contrary to popular belief learning more information is not what makes people successful. It is in your moments of decision that your destiny is shaped." There are plenty of highly intelligent people that never achieve anything above mediocrity. Successful people do not delay making decisions, especially important ones. They weigh the options and make the most informed choices, but they do not procrastinate with this process. A successful person is able to be decisive because they have a clear vision of where they are going. Therefore, they are able to tell whether or not decisions are in alignment with that vision. Quite often it is the decisions that you don't make that can hurt you the most. You must realize that no decision at all is still a decision. This lack of attention greatly impacts your life. A person ends up broke at retiring age because they never made the decision to be financially free. A person ends up overweight and out of shape because they never decided to make health and fitness a must. A person ends up divorced because they never made a decision to constantly nurture the relationship.

One of the reasons why people avoid this process is because the fear of making the wrong decision is so deeply embedded in most people. As the saying goes, "death kills a person one time, but fear kills a person over and over again. The fear of failure kills countless dreams and splendid plans." However, the truly successful person understands that a certain amount of failure is necessary in order to succeed, and so they take the actions regardless of the fear. They are normally no less fearful than the unsuccessful person, but they act in spite of fear and learn what they need to make the necessary adjustments as they go along.

True success comes from making decisions and backing them up with massive action. People who make conscious decisions have much richer lives than those who don't because they tend to try more things. Tony Robbins has a quote that sums this up. It says, "The quality of a person's life is in direct proportion to the amount of uncertainty they can handle." Decision making takes you out of paralysis of analysis. It moves energy forward by increasing your clarity because it forces you to think things out. Even situations where you decide not to do something move you forward because you are strengthening your focus. Therefore, embrace this process because with each decision you are building a muscle that will make you more effective in every area of your life.

Action Steps for Decision Making

1. Determine from this day forward to be a decision maker.

2. Always base your choices on whether the decision aligns with your vision.

3. When fear comes up about making the wrong decision, simply accept that fear is a natural part of the decision-making process and make the most informed choice you can without overanalyzing.

#51   Direction

Direction. Where are you now? Where are you going? Are you on pace to get it? What's next in your life? Have you ever been at the point where you knew you needed to do something a little differently but were not quite sure what? There is a saying that goes "the number one reason why people don't get what they want is that they don't know what they want." Clarity is true power. It is what gives your life purpose and enables you to harness your focus. If clarity is not present you lose energy, confidence, and fulfillment. Whenever you get to this point, ask your inner genie the essential question. The essential question is "if a genie said you could have whatever you want and create whatever your heart desires, and time and money are not factors, what would you ask for?" We all have an inner genie. You may call it consciousness, your soul, spirit, or intuition. The name is not as important as the understanding and the use of it is.

Therefore, however you refer to it, when you are trying to figure out what direction to go in next, pose the essential question. It is the essential question because it frees the mind from two of the biggest blocks that we so often say are the reasons for not following our hearts, and they are time and money. Shakti Gawain said, "Every time you don't follow your own inner guidance, you feel a loss of energy, loss of power, a sense of spiritual deadness." Always remember if you are truly committed to something and you are flexible in your approach then time and money are not really a factor, because you will find a way to create the time, and you will figure out a way to get the money. Another great quote by Tony Robbins says, "The only thing preventing you from having everything you want are your stories and reasons about why you can't have it." The essential question will also enable you to naturally sense what needs to be next in your life without acting out of obligation or from someone else's opinion of what you should be doing.

ACTION STEPS FOR DETERMINING YOUR DIRECTION

1. Make a decision to always trust your intuition when determining any direction.

2. Any time you find yourself frustrated, flustered, or unsure of your life's direction, ask the essential question, "If a genie said you can have whatever you want or create whatever your heart desires, and time and money are not factors, what would you ask for?"

3. Once you are clear about your direction, write out a plan to get there. Have the plan be as simple and straightforward as possible. Then schedule your plan and work on it in some way every day.

#52 Energy

Energy. All the strategies that are talked about in this book presuppose that you have the energy to apply them. Most of us have a big list of things on our already full plates that must be done in addition to working on our goals and dream projects. Surely you have bills to pay, jobs to attend, and families to be with, but in most cases, after taking care of those areas you have nothing left to put into yourself. Therefore, it is important to know how to generate energy.

Exercise of course is a great way. Meditation is also very good because it reconnects you to your source, which naturally energizes you. Deep breathing is important because it regenerates the cells with oxygen. Diet is also very important because it is your fuel for the day. Eating foods that are very high in water content, such as fruits and vegetables, is a tremendous energizer. Bear in mind that the body is made up of more than 75 percent water and the brain is made up of 85 percent water, so by simply drinking lots of water, ideally half your body weight in ounces, you increase your energy level.

Also realize that sweets and foods that clog you, such as cheese and other dairy products or processed foods, decrease your energy level. Even though these foods may taste good and provide a temporary high, they will always bring you back down. It is also important to look to avoid the three whites as much as possible.

They are white flour, white salt, and white sugar. If you are going to do them, then moderation is the key.

In looking to optimize your wellness, understand that the energy from fruits and vegetables, especially when they are served in fresh juices will provide you with energy boosts with greater longevity. This is especially true of green juices because they alkalize the blood and oxygenate the cells. If you could just do two green juices a day, lots of water, and a salad with each meal, you would notice a significant increase in your energy level just from doing these three things. Lastly, nothing beats a good night's sleep. The more rested you are, the more motivated you will be.

ACTIONS STEPS FOR ENERGIZING

1. Exercise at least three to four times a week in a way that increases the heart rate.

    Meditate daily, and focus on deep breathing from your diaphragm during your meditation and throughout your day.

2. Increase your water intake to half your body weight in ounces daily.

    Work toward eating a salad with each meal and as many greens as possible in the form of juices, salads, and vitamin and mineral supplements daily.

3. Log what you put into your body each day in order to have balance with your food, and strive for eight hours of sleep per night.

#53 Focus and Accountability

Focus and accountability. As human beings we have the ability to focus our energy like laser beams. This type of concentration is necessary in order to accomplish anything. Yet even though we all have this special power, how many people consistently get themselves to use it? There are a number of ways to do this. Many of these have already been mentioned in this book, such as writing down a plan, visualizing, etc.

However, knowing what to do and actually doing it are two very different ball games. Having clarity about your intention, strong enough reasons to follow through, and consistently doing inner work are all major pieces of the puzzle. Yet after all these ingredients are in place, then your ability to follow through on what you know to do is a large part of what makes the difference between success and failure. It has been said that "80 percent of success is simply showing up"— in other words, getting into action. So the big question becomes how do you get yourself to make sure you that you follow through and use these tools to focus? How do you ensure that you follow through on the plan that you have created in order to hit your mark? Henry Ford said, "Obstacles are those frightful things you see when you take your eyes off your goals."

A great way to keep your focus is by getting coaching or working within a mastermind group in which everyone supports one another toward accomplishing their goals. If you choose not to use either one of these options, then you can connect with someone like a friend or acquaintance on a weekly basis who you tell your commitments to. The other person can also tell you their commitments if they choose, so that you both benefit from the exchange. By continually working together in a spirit of personal harmony, both people experience greater levels of enthusiasm, faith, action, and courage than if they were attempting to accomplish their goals by themselves.

This is an extremely powerful way of raising your standards by holding yourself accountable. To an extent, some pressure is good because it makes it more difficult for you to stray off course, which is much easier if you are working by yourself. You are much less apt to be distracted by television, phone calls, or anything else if you know that someone is going to ask you for a progress report. Having this kind of support structure in place will have you demand more from yourself. When you study patterns of success, you will notice that the most successful people have strong teams of people under them in the form of coaches, advisors, etc., and they have higher standards than average people do. Because successful people are willing to pay the price to meet these standards, they enjoy all the rewards that come with high achievement. These rewards are available for anyone. Simply model and mirror these patterns and you will have the same results.

ACTION STEPS TO CREATE FOCUS AND ACCOUNTABILITY

1. Absolutely make the very important decision to get a personal coach to support you with your goals.

2. A second option is to create a mastermind group with other like-minded people for additional energy, focus, ideas, and networking.

3. If you already are working with someone then you can increase your focus by upping the frequency with which you speak to them and give them your tasks.

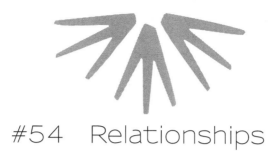

#54 Relationships

Relationships. It has been said that "the purpose of relationships is to magnify the human experience." Life becomes much richer when we can cultivate meaningful relationships with people. Studies show relationships are responsible for at least 85 percent of our happiness or unhappiness in life. That is a huge percentage. The ability to create extraordinary relationships in your life is an important skill. One of the most important keys to amazing relationships is unconditional love. Love is the most powerful force in the universe, and when you can give it without all the attachments about how other people are going to respond, you are able to be happily detached from others and to remain connected to your source. This is truly living in your power. It ensures that you bring your light to every relationship. The Dai Lai Lama said, "Remember that the best relationship is one in which your love for each other exceeds your need for each other." As a result others will be touched by your light, and it will bring out the best in them. When you relate from unconditional love, your very presence will make people feel better about themselves.

The challenge for most people is that they do not practice the golden rule of relationships. The golden rule of relationships is that whatever it is you want, you must be, do, have, and give first. First you must give it to yourself, because you cannot give what you don't have. In other words you must fill up your own cup before you fill up someone else's. The second piece of this golden rule of relationships is that you then must be the first one to give to other people what you want without waiting for them to give it to you first. In other words if you want love, respect, attention, and compassion, you must give all of those things to yourself first and then give all those same qualities to the other person without waiting to first receive it from them.

Another key to great relationships is to let go of the need to be right. Some of us would rather die than be proven wrong. We just know that we are right, and we feel that if the other person just understood that then everything would be as it is supposed to be. Warning: when you are thinking this way, you are being run by your ego—not your highest self—and it is impossible to be at peace when you operate from your ego. As the saying goes, "you can either be right or in love."

Try the mind-set that neither person is right or wrong, just different. However, the other person is seeing the world is based on their own perspective. We all look at life based on our own unique conditioning and experiences. If we put our judgments aside and really listen by putting ourselves in the other person's world, then we can understand them, and we might learn a thing or two as well. As Stephen Covey said, "Seek first to understand."

This is requires an ability to simply let go of the need to control. It means being in a space where you are at peace with the other person and their actions. This does not mean that you condone everything that they do or that you don't communicate and work toward certain objectives but that you love the person unconditionally for who they are and who they aren't.

ACTION STEPS FOR GREAT RELATIONSHIPS

1. Determine that you will continue to fine-tune your ability to create extraordinary relationships by constantly studying, visualizing, affirming, etc.

2. Practice the golden rule of relationships, especially focusing on unconditional love.

3. Release the need to be right and seek to understand the other person's perspective first.

#55 Adversity

Adversity. Adversity is your friend. Most of the time when a difficult situation arises we are angered or annoyed by it. This is only because of our limited outlook. Instead of looking at the challenge as a great opportunity, we take on the mind-set that this should not be happening. However, in looking at it this way we are causing ourselves unnecessary pain. There is absolutely positively nothing that happens in this world that is not supposed to occur, including your desire to change a situation. Everything happens exactly the way it was supposed to whether we want to believe it or not. The key is viewing the incident in such a way that it empowers us.

We live in a loving and supportive universe. As the saying goes, "When the great creator wants to give you a present, it is quite often wrapped up in the form of a problem." Successful people have an underlying belief that they are destined to be a success in their lives and that everything that happens to them is leading them to that success. Confucius said, "The gem cannot be polished without friction, nor man perfected without trials." If you don't have this mind-set you will miss the lesson and the blessing in every challenge. When this happens the universe will create a situation for you with even more impact so that you can actually get the message.

As Napoleon Hill said, "For every negative situation look for the seed of an equivalent benefit." This kind of viewpoint takes tremendous discipline because we are so used to looking at things, both big and small, like they shouldn't be. If we change our sense of perception, then we will not only grow and expand with every challenge, but we will find benefits that we never would have realized were there otherwise. Most importantly we will be at peace with whatever happens to us.

ACTION STEPS TO MOVE THROUGH ADVERSITY

1. Determine that you will be a huge success in your life and make a decision to embrace adversity instead of resisting it.

2. Give thanks for every challenge that comes in your life, for it is providing you with an opportunity to master yourself and stretch outside of your comfort zone.

3. With every adversity that you experience, ask yourself "How can I actually use the situation to move me closer to realizing my intention?"

#56 Visualization

Visualization. Without a doubt this is one of the most underrated tools for achievement. The most successful people in any field have learned how to tap into the deeper recesses of the mind so as to fulfill their dreams. Mental imagery, which is the natural language of the right brain and the subconscious, is a tool that has been around since 60,000 BC. Ancient Shaman masters would use this tool in order to have successful hunts.

This intriguing use of imagery has been used by athletes, executives, inventors, and everyday people to program the mind to accomplish their goals. Visualization has been used to promote healing, to nurture relationships, create inventions, perform at very high levels, and create many other kinds of transformation. Roger Bannister, the man who broke the four-minute mile in 1954, attributed his success to the mental rehearsals that he would do religiously on a daily basis. Through conditioning your mind through visualization, you are using imagination to mentally rehearse the results you want in life.

As Dr. Lee Pulos, PhD, says, "you are tapping into your conscious and subconscious mind and having them work in unison in such a way that they create a self-fulfilling prophecy." Psychologists estimate that one hour of visualization is the equivalent of seven hours of work. This tool is so simple that its power is often overlooked. Yet this process is mentioned in countless self-development books. It is the equivalent of pressing a magic button for anything that you want in your life. For any goal or challenge that you would like to get to or move through, this is just a sign and a signal that you need to spend more time visualizing yourself having the result you want. Remember that your outer world is just a reflection and manifestation of your inner world. It is impossible to have a shift with your outer results unless you have a shift internally first. Pay attention to the signs that you need to condition yourself for the success you desire. You will always be able to tell your predominant programming by simply observing your results. Create the proper mental programming necessary in order to accomplish your goals by using this amazing tool daily. The effects of the process are immediate. If you just used this one tool every single day and ignored every other technique and principle in this book, it could very well be enough to get you to where you want to be.

ACTION STEPS FOR VISUALIZATION

1. Every day visualize for at least twenty minutes. Visualize for at least ten minutes first thing in the morning, seeing your perfect day, week, month, and year with all your goals being realized. Repeat the process again in the evening.

2. Visualize anything that you are struggling with at the moment, like getting out of bed, working out, completing a project, an important communication, etc. See yourself going through the motions and then having the end result.

3. Make sure that your visualizations are as consistent and detailed as possible and, most importantly, full of the great emotions you expect to experience when you have realized your desired result. Even if the emotions feel forced, make believe that they are very real, and eventually they will be.

#57 Perspective and Meaning

Perspective and meaning. Many people have heard the term "life is what you make it," but have you ever considered that life is as you see it. We tend to view the world as we are inside. If you are very thirsty and someone brings you a drink of water that is filled to the middle, is the glass half empty or half full? The response to this question really depends on the person who is answering it and their point of view. Both answers could be perceived as accurate, but which outlook is the most beneficial to the respondent? Another scenario, you are interacting with a friend, acquaintance, or family member, and for as long as you can remember this person's behavior has been edgy and irritable. Do you label this person a jerk or as someone who is struggling with some issues in their life? Neither answer is right or wrong because a strong case could be made for each side, but which point of view would be more useful to have? The second viewpoint enables you to come from a more compassionate and spiritual place, which means you will be at peace. This doesn't even mean that you have to spend time with the person, but it does mean that regardless, your energy will be in a higher place.

Our lives literally mean whatever we decide they mean. At first, hearing this concept may seem a bit off base. However, when you really think about it, all that you do and experience ends up being interpreted by you. Yet many of your interpretations can end up being negative ones, especially when a situation is challenging. Winston Churchill said, "A pessimist sees the difficulty in every opportunity; an optimist sees the opportunity in every difficulty."

What happens when a person does something differently from how you would like them to? How does this affect you? Tony Robbins said that "feelings are the result of what we focus on and the meaning we give it." Put another way, "nothing has meaning except for the meaning we give it." This wisdom points out that everything is all made up. It may be a fact that something has literally occurred in your life, but you decide whether that something is good or bad, right or wrong, valuable or worthless. Human beings are "meaning-making machines." It is what we do. There is really no need to fight or resist this law of nature.

We ascribe meaning to everything. This pattern can be empowering or very destructive, depending on the how it is used. In other words you are the one who determines what something means, and since you are going to give the situation a meaning anyway, you may as well give it a meaning that is going to strengthen you. This is a powerful way to direct your focus. As complex and amazing as we are, human beings can pretty much only focus on one thing at a time. Even when you are multitasking, you are still giving energy to one thing in each moment. As simplistic as this may seem, it is one of your greatest gifts. The ability to determine what something means in your life and how you are going to respond and use it is what makes you uniquely human. As Charles Swindoll says, "We cannot change our past. We cannot change the fact that people will act in a certain way. We cannot change the inevitable. The only thing we can do is play on the one string we have, and that is our attitude. I am convinced that life is 10 percent what happens to me and 90 percent how I react to it. And so it is with you."

You always have a choice of what to think, and if your choice of meaning leaves you feeling angry, guilty, shameful, victimized or bad in any way, then you need to shift your perspective. We are not put on this earth to be feeling bad. Everything, including the challenges we experience, are for our growth and happiness. In his work *The Science of Personal Achievement*, Napoleon Hill said,

"For every negative situation look for the seed of an equivalent benefit." If you are always feeling bad, then you are constantly creating meaning that disconnects you from your higher power and you are missing the value in the situation. Your higher power, God, spirit, consciousness, or whatever you choose to call it is a force that is steeped in love. Because of this you can tell if you are connected to it if your interpretations of life have you regularly experiencing that love.

ACTION STEPS FOR AN EMPOWERING PERSPECTIVE AND MEANING

1. As a rule of thumb, practice taking on the perspective which makes you stronger and leaves you at peace with each situation. Apply this principle by creating meanings that allow you to be light, humorous, and to greet everyone with love and respect.

2. If you find that you are stuck in low energy because of how you are interpreting a situation, as Tony Robbins said, "change your process or your procedure." This means that you either change the way you look at the situation, change your actions, or change both.

3. "For every negative situation or experience look for the seed of an equivalent benefit." Ask yourself the question "How can I use this experience to further my mission and to reach my goals?" This practice takes tremendous discipline because most people are prone toward the negative. Like any new muscle it must be strengthened over time, yet the rewards from practicing this way of being are priceless.

#58   Habit

Habit. What keeps you from experiencing all that you desire? When you see others who appear to have accomplished or obtained what you want, do you take note of how they got there? What separates you from this person whom you so admire? What is it that has enabled them to have what you wish for? There is a saying that goes "if someone has something that you want, they know something that you don't." Find out what that is by studying, modeling, and mirroring them. What is it that distinguishes them from the rest of the pack?

The answer is habit. It is estimated that 80 percent of your thoughts and actions are habitual. You have virtually limitless potential. However, a great deal of this potential goes untapped because of your habits. Since you are destined to fall prey to your habits, develop ones that will mint gold. Curb your appetites to please the senses excessively through eating, sleeping, drinking, and foster habits that will have you truly love and empower yourself.

It can take about thirty days straight to create a new habit. Remember if you created one new habit a month for twelve months, then by the end of that year you would be a vastly more effective person. It may seem that these would only be minor changes, but cumulatively they would greatly alter the course of your life. For example, what if one of your habits for the month was to begin the practice of saving and investing at least one hundred dollars a month.

If you were to start this at the age of twenty-five and invest it in a solid mutual or index fund, and you never invested more than one hundred dollars a month, but you did this until you were sixty-five, then by retiring age you would have just over a million dollars from this practice alone. On the other hand, if you never started this small habit, you would most likely end up broke by retiring age like the vast majority of people do. Good habits, whether they are big or small, over the long haul make a world of difference. The key is to create the habit one small step at a time.

ACTION STEPS FOR CREATING STRONG HABITS

1. As always, with every goal and situation, be crystal clear about what it is you want.

2. Ask yourself which habits would be most beneficial for realizing your intention if you were to develop them.

3. Build your habits in small increments, taking on one per month. The following month continue to work your new habit, and then incorporate an additional one on top of it. Initially this will be uncomfortable, but this is the only way to grow, and eventually it will become one of the most valuable practices of your life.

#59   The Law of Attraction

The law of attraction. This is one of the most powerful, popular, and misunderstood laws of the universe. You are totally responsible for what is showing up in your life. This is not how most of us have been trained to think. We mistakenly feel that something or someone is usually at fault for our lack of results or our present situation. You are the one who creates your life through your thoughts, words, actions, and feelings. It may seem as if some things just randomly happen to you, but this is not a random universe. It works with pinpoint precision. Even the seemingly coincidental occurrences are being attracted to you. Whether a situation is extremely challenging or absolutely delightful, you are attracting it in to your life based on your level of energy and vibration. The universe is giving you very valuable messages, lessons, and blessings with each experience. You can continue to expand your capacity to enjoy more of life's abundance by continually deepening your understanding and raising your energy level.

One of the main reasons why successful people are successful is because they take full responsibility for every aspect of their lives and devote the majority of their attention to what it is they want in life. As Brian Tracy said, "You become what you think about most of the time." The principles of attraction are definitely metaphysical, meaning they are not so readily visible to the naked eye. As T. Harv Eker said, "What you cannot see is far more powerful than what you can see." Napoleon Hill added, "The mind is like a rich garden spot, in that it will produce whatever is planted there." The mind attracts the material equivalent of whatever it focuses on.

It bears repeating the often-used words of "like attracts like" and "water seeks its own level." This is why it is important to monitor your thoughts and only think about what you want, because these thoughts go into your subconscious and greatly impact not only what actions you take but also what mental energy you are sending out into the world. In this way the mind is like an open broadcasting and receiving unit. It will tune in to the thoughts of others that are in alignment with the thoughts it sends out. The tricky part is that this is also true for negative thoughts. Which means you cannot spend substantial time worrying or thinking about the things that you do not want, because you will begin to materialize them in your life. Again Napoleon Hill reminds us "You must be so busy thinking and working towards the things you want that you don't have time to think about what you don't want."

ACTION STEPS FOR USING THE LAW OF ATTRACTION

1. Always visualize, affirm, write, and meditate on your goals and intentions daily so you continually raise your energy and frequency level.

2. Make sure that your thoughts, words, actions, and feelings are in harmony with your aspirations so that you stay in alignment with your source and your purpose.

3. Pay close attention to the feedback the universe is giving you, and make the necessary adjustments in your way of being so that you get the lesson and the blessing in every experience.

#60 Commitment

Commitment. In order to excel or succeed in any venue, commitment is critical. Yet how do you know if you are committed? At what point can you tell if you have this drive or not? As our great friend Tony Robbins said, "The answer lies with your musts." This means people tend to get whatever they feel they absolutely must have. This is a very different frame of mind from simply feeling that it would be nice to have something. When a goal is merely nice, it normally does not have enough energy behind it to be realized because you are not totally willing to do your part to create it. At this level, the desire is not strong enough for you to consider yourself committed.

When you are committed, despite whatever fear, worry, or other crippling feelings might come up, your attitude is one in which you are going to accomplish your goal no matter what it takes because you must have it. In short you have made a decision to be unstoppable despite any unforeseen obstacles that may come your way. To be committed, you cannot be iffy. You cannot stay on the fence. There can be no reservations. If reservations do come up, they are overpowered by your hunger to realize your outcome. Few people are able to get themselves to this point with their goals, but successful people always do. Successful people do this regularly. In fact they don't know any other way to live their lives. Because they are so accustomed to success and they know that this is the only way to get it, commitment becomes their pathway of least resistance.

The only way to emotionally get to this place of true commitment is to have strong-enough reasons for why you want something. There is a saying that goes "if you have a big enough why, the how will take care of itself." Take some time to think about how it will cost you if you don't realize your commitment and all the ways it will benefit you when you do. If this process doesn't make your goal a must, either change your reasons or change your goal.

Action Steps for Creating Commitment

1. Think about something that you have been wishy-washy about that you want, and make it a must. Do this with the realization that true commitment is one of the first steps to opening up the pathways of success.

2. Create this sense of urgency by coming up with a list of ten costs for not accomplishing your goal and ten payoffs for completing it. Make sure the list uses very descriptive words to describe the costs and benefits in order to create strong emotional responses.

3. Put this list where you can see and review it daily. Take action every day to realize your intention and do not give up until you have accomplished it or something better.

#61   Outlook on the World

Outlook on the world. How do you view yourself in relation to everyone else? Where do you fit in the full scheme of things? Do you see yourself as being separate from all that is going on around you? What are your typical responses to the people you are surrounded by? Your perception of the world and where you fit in it determine your day-to-day emotions as well as the level of harmony you experience in your life. Most people tend to see themselves as significant, special, and separate from the rest of the world. Again as mentioned before, this is the ego. Yes, we are each unique, but we are not special by way of being separate. You are an individual as well as someone who is connected to the larger whole. This is the same larger whole that unites all of us. When you are able to see how you are one with the larger whole that surrounds you, it is easier to be at peace.

Once you have integrated this understanding into your life, you are able to be less judgmental and more free. Judgment creates inner turmoil. When you are able to exist without it, you no longer need to constantly prove your own worth. Instead you are able to look at the behavior of others with detachment. This doesn't mean that you don't care or don't have things to contribute to the world; it is having faith that each person has their own path and their own karma that they must deal with. This approach helps you to relinquish control and be able to flow with any circumstances that come your way. This also helps you be more open to receive life's abundance, because you are not blocked with anger. Remember this sentence from the Siddha Yoga teachings: "When you are judging others, you can not be in the presence of your own love." The great Siddha Master Gurumayi beautifully explained this when she said, "As long as the mind does not rest in the heart it gives birth to illusory worlds and illusory concepts. An untrained mind is constantly agitated. However, when the mind rests in the heart, all barriers break down, and it experiences immense consciousness. Therefore, it is the duty of a seeker to constantly bring the mind continually back to its source." Determine to practice this approach to life and notice the increase in joy and success that you experience as a result.

ACTION STEPS FOR CREATING AN IDEAL OUTLOOK ON THE WORLD

1. See yourself as connected to everything around you instead of just as an individual.

2. On a daily basis ask and answer the question "How may I serve?" This applies to you and your world.

3. Anytime you notice that you are out of balance due to lower energy feelings of anger or frustration, etc., take a minute to breathe deeply, gather yourself, and return to a place of love. Do this by continually searching for the good in each situation.

#62   Self-Expression

Self-expression. Are you fully self-expressed? Are you one with your inner voice, such that you listen to its dictates always, even when others strongly disagree? Do you sometimes not say something for fear of how others will view you even though your inner urge is to speak? Do you not attempt certain fun activities, projects, or classes because you fear messing up or looking bad? What about your choices of clothing? Do you ever stifle your creativity in this area so you don't look strange to people?

Just as we are all one and connected, we all have unique gifts that we are meant to share in our lifetime. As T. Harv Eker said, "Life is like one giant potluck dinner, and we each bring something different to the table." It has been said that when we don't self-express by using our unique talents, then at least a thousand other people miss out. This means that at least a thousand other people will not share their unique gifts with the world because they need to experience our gifts in order to release their own. This puts a very different perspective on self-expression. It takes it from being the common misconception of something that is egotistical to something that actually allows you to share your gifts.

Self-expression is significant for two reasons. For one, it supports your unique contributions to the world no matter how big or small they may be. The second reason is that it has you be centered in your life because you are listening to and following your inner compass instead of living life based on other people's fears, judgments, and opinions. Gandhi said, "Happiness is when what you think, what you say, and what you do are in harmony." All self-development work is ultimately about fine-tuning your ability to listen to your intuition with every decision. These decisions range from what livelihood you choose all the way down to which pair of shoes you pick out for the day. When you listen to your intuition in this way, it gives you confidence, a feeling of control, and purpose. Your energy will rise and your self-concept will expand because you will like how you are being in the world. When you ignore your intuition it drains your energy, making you more tired. It also decreases your confidence, and ultimately it will destroy you. To paraphrase the Bible, "when you express what is inside of you it will set you free, and if you don't express what is in you, then it will tear you apart from the inside."

Self-expression is what makes the world rich. In all of time there will never ever be another you. As it said in Og Mandino's classic *The Greatest Salesman in the World*, "I am rare and there is value in all rarity; therefore, I am valuable."

ACTION STEPS FOR SELF-EXPRESSION

1. Understand that your self-expression is a gift to you and the world.

2. Practice listening to your intuition every day by meditating, journaling, and having quiet time.

3. Once you are clear about the guidance your intuition is giving you, trust it and express yourself by following through on what it is telling you, despite any fear, uncertainty, or resistance from anyone, including yourself.

#63 Persistence

Persistence. Have you ever had a goal that you were working toward and it just didn't seem to be working out? No matter what you did or how good your idea was, things were just not clicking? Did you quit at that point? Strangely enough, it is those times when we think we have reached our threshold and we can't go any further that it is crucial to keep going. Persistence is necessary for success in any calling. We tend to feel like we are the only ones who have gone through this type of hardship, but in truth everyone that we admire has had to move through this process in some way or another. It is part of paying your dues. It is what tests your faith and a major part of the price you must pay for any success.

Persistence is the principle that states that anything that is really worth it, will at times take a great deal of effort. Lack of persistence is why so many people fail. The majority of people simply run out of hope. However, as Les Brown said, "If you get knocked down on your back, remember that if you can look up, you can get up." There is always something more you can do to put the odds in your favor. Ask yourself what were you not willing to do to have what you wanted? Og Mandino said it best when he said, "If your determination to win is big enough, then you will succeed, and you must fail often to succeed only once."

The other important aspect of persistence is what it will make of you. Realizing a goal or intention is not just for the mere sake of the goal, but also for who you have to become in the process. Persistence is a characteristic of greatness. Yet without it greatness is impossible. Persistence is not always comfortable, but it is necessary. Persistence will test you, but it will also reward you. It can pull you through the harshest rains but lead you to the greatest sunset. Calvin Coolidge has a famous quote that beautifully sums this up: "Nothing in the world can take the place of persistence. Talent will not; nothing is more common than unsuccessful people with talent. Genius will not; unrewarded genius is almost a proverb. Education will not; the world is full of educated derelicts. Persistence and determination alone are omnipotent."

What you want wants you just as much, and it deserves your energy, faith, and persistence to obtain it.

ACTION STEPS FOR PERSISTENCE

1. Notice the pattern of persistence in the people that have what you want, and model that same pattern in your endeavors.

2. Visualize and affirm the qualities of persistence in yourself every day first thing in the morning. Also visualize this quality in the moments during the day when you are struggling or feel weak. See yourself persisting successfully.

3. Today, recommit to something that you thought was a lost cause and start to strengthen your persistence muscle, for the next time you push may be the one where you break through.

#64　Seize the Day

Carpe diem. This is a Latin term that means "seize the day." There are a couple of ways to interpret this phrase. It can mean live and be present in the moment. It could also mean make every second count, or these words could simply be interpreted as "live this day as if it is your last." Whichever meaning you use, it is important to get the core message here, and that is to be fully aware and engaged in your experience right now. When you don't do this, you lose your life. This happens when you have disconnected from the joy and uniqueness of that particular moment in your existence. A signal that you are running this pattern is when you are either overly focused on your future or dwelling in the past. When you are frozen by fear, constantly burdening yourself with what you think you "should" do, and feeling obligated to engage in something, then you have lost some sight of what your intention is in that present moment. This way of being becomes a pattern that ultimately prevents you from fully experiencing your life.

How would you live your life if you knew you were dying? What things would you make more of a priority? What things would you release? What communications would you make? Answering these questions gives you the perspective that is necessary for truly seizing the day. In a sense, you are dying. No one is promised another day. If you live your life like someday you will get around to the things that really matter to you, then you will not be fully engaged and fulfilled in your life. Tony Robbins said, "The road called someday leads to a town called nowhere."

Once you are pursuing intentions that are truly worthwhile, it is important to fully enjoy them. If you are so busy looking toward the end result then you miss the journey, which is where you will spend most of your time. Don't wait until you have accomplished some goal before you allow yourself to experience all the joy that you anticipate will come with that goal. Instead, create that emotional state now, while you are engaged in the process and as a result you will attract that outcome to you much more quickly because you will be a vibrational match with it. You cannot attract anything into your life that you are not a vibrational match with. Therefore, one of the best ways to "seize the day" is to raise your vibration by performing every action from the joy of your life's purpose. This is where you will experience true greatness in your life.

ACTION STEPS TO SEIZE THE DAY

1. Ask yourself what you would do if you found out you only had one year left to live.

2. Write down your answers and notice if any of them are vastly different from the predominant direction your life is going in now. Are there any dreams that you have released that you still need to pick up in some way?

3. If there are any inconsistencies between where you are and where you ideally want to be, then write out a clear goal, deadline, and plan for each intention which you begin following immediately.

#65   Listening

Listening. How well do you listen? How well are you listening right now? Most of us tend to think we are great listeners, but if we were to ask those closest to us what they thought, the answer might be very different. Listening is significant for a number of different reasons. A person needs to know how to listen to those around them, how to listen to their inner urges, and how to pay attention to the many signals the universe sends them. It is only through being silent that we can receive this information. People normally have a great deal more to say, then they are willing to absorb.

Again much of this is due to the ego. We often feel that we have to constantly talk, justify, compete, or impress. It is important to be mindful of these urges because they often disconnect us from others and ourselves. A person will not be able to listen well to others if they cannot first listen well to themselves when they are alone. As Swami Chidvilasananda said, "The tongue weighs very little, but so few can hold it." Les Brown put it this way: "God gave us two ears and one mouth so we must learn to listen twice as much as we speak."

Most "problems" in human relations stem from a block in communication. It has been said that "every communication is either an expression of love or a cry for help." And in order to dissolve these boundaries we must follow Steven Covey's fifth habit, which says, "Seek first to understand, then be understood." When you are listening to someone you ideally want to make them feel like the most important person in the world at that moment. This is actually a great gift you are giving to the person. It gives them a feeling of being valued. It increases their self-worth. It establishes trust. You cannot connect with someone unless they trust you. When you have shown a willingness to drop your agenda or perspective and put yourself in the other person's shoes, you have demonstrated that you sincerely care about the other person. When a person knows that you feel this way then they are able to be vulnerable and have trust in you. The bottom line is, without listening, there can be no trust, and without trust you cannot have a positive influence on people.

If you can fine-tune this tool, you won't believe the kinds of insights you will begin to have. Many of your questions will be answered, and you will start to see the hundreds of messages that the universe sends daily to guide and protect you. It will become easier for you to hear and trust your intuition. Also one of the greatest human needs is that of being heard and understood. We feel connected when this happens. When someone feels listened to, they feel important. One of the best ways to raise a person's mood, energy, and self-concept is to really listen to them. Yet you can only give someone this gift when you are fully taking in what they are saying, such that you genuinely understand where the other person is coming from. So start honing your ability to listen today, and if you are curious to find out what kind of a listener you are, the best way is to ask the people who you interact with the most. You may be surprised by the answers.

ACTION STEPS FOR GREAT LISTENING

1. When you are listening to someone make sure that you are making strong and consistent eye contact with them while they are talking. Focus on them like they are the most important person in the world.

2. Slightly lean your head in toward the person so you zero in on what they are saying. Nod your head to demonstrate that you are receiving the information.

3. Occasionally during the conversation reflect back to the person who is speaking to you what they have just said in your own words to make sure you fully absorbed it. After reflecting, wait for them to acknowledge that you heard them correctly. If not then ask them to clarify and reflect back to them again until they confirm you heard them correctly.

#66 Embrace Discomfort

Embrace discomfort. Hands down one of the biggest reasons why people fail at anything is an unwillingness to be uncomfortable. The unsuccessful person shies away from discomfort while the successful person embraces it. No one inherently likes to be uncomfortable, because as human beings we are wired to move away from pain and toward pleasure. However, a successful person has an overwhelmingly strong emotional connection to the pleasure of the end result. That pleasure by far outweighs the discomfort they will have to go through in order to achieve the end result.

This is why it is absolutely critical to develop strong emotional reasons as to why something is important for you to have or achieve. Since it is guaranteed that you will have to get uncomfortable in order to succeed, you need to do the inner work ahead of time or else you will not have what it takes to take the necessary action. Comfort kills ambitions, dreams, and potential. So many people avoid various tasks because they mistakenly think that they have to wait for it to be more comfortable for them to know that the time is right. This misconception can cost you your life. It will not necessarily terminate your existence, but it can have you living in such a way that you feel dead inside. Again, your natural state of being is growth, and you are only growing when you are expanding out of your regular way of being, your comfort zone.

If you were to do a study on the highest achievers in any field, you would see that this is a very common trait. These people have cemented the habit of doing the uncomfortable. They have demonstrated the pattern of doing over and over again what the failures simply refuse to do. They don't like it any more than the unsuccessful person, but they are so wired internally for success that nothing will stop them from constantly doing whatever it takes. It doesn't mean that they always do it in balance, but they have conditioned themselves to dive into what has to be done. Hence, they regularly experience the best that life has to offer because this way of being for them is a habit.

And so it is with you. Most people refuse to get uncomfortable because it brings up so many different issues for them. Sure they don't want to be uncomfortable, but on a deeper level they don't want to fail, succeed, look bad, feel they deserve what they want, or want to have to face their fears. As the saying goes, "if you do the thing you fear, the death of that fear is certain." Yes, this is uncomfortable, but it is temporary and pales in comparison to a life that is unfulfilled. Ultimately embracing your discomfort will lead you to your greatest life. This can be difficult, but it is the price you have to pay for your success and abundance, and who you develop into as a result is more than worth it.

Action Steps for Embracing Discomfort

1. Constantly reinforce the understanding that in order to be successful you must get uncomfortable.

2. Strengthen this muscle in yourself daily by doing the things that scare you the most that will progress your goals.

3. Reinforce this habit by always deliberately rewarding the uncomfortable activity.

#67   Loving Yourself

Loving yourself. Most of us tend to think that in order to perform better we must be hard on ourselves. We think it is more productive to beat ourselves up than it is to be loving. Again we must remember Julia Cameron's words from *The Artist's Way*: "Treating yourself like a precious object will make you strong." These words are a perfect reminder that love is the most powerful force in the universe. Let's take a closer look at exactly how you can love yourself more. To begin with, always remember that you cannot love anyone else unless you love yourself first. This goes for family, friends, acquaintances, and anyone else. "You cannot give what you don't have," as Wayne Dyer said. In this way it is important to fill your cup up so you have more to share. Most people think they will fully love themselves when they have accomplished everything they want or that it is okay to love themselves a little bit, but only after they have catered to everyone else. This is backward. Start with loving yourself first, and the rest will happen more easily. This doesn't mean that you are not mindful or considerate of others; it simply means that in order serve at the highest level you must feel and be at the highest level. Doing this requires an awareness of what it takes to mentally, spiritually, emotionally, and physically be at your best.

Loving yourself covers a lot of ground. It means getting the proper rest. It means allowing yourself downtime just for you. It means pursuing your dreams. It means doing some of your favorite activities, eating your favorite foods, while at the same time making sure your body gets the proper nourishment for fuel and energy. A big word that needs to be used in this process is pampering. Take a day or weekend to plan a bunch of fun activities. Go to a fun movie, museum, or sporting event. Get a manicure or massage or go for a walk in the park. Go bowling. Buy yourself some flowers. Making these things a priority does not mean that you have lowered your standards or that you are any less disciplined. To the contrary they mean that you are a balanced person. Believe it or not, doing all of these things make it easier for you to work more effectively. It is easier to work harder when you have had fun. When your inner child is pleased, it will not throw a temper tantrum when it is time to work. You will be less resistant and more motivated. You will also be vibrating on the frequency of the things you desire. As Rhonda Byrne said, "You cannot attract the things you would love to have in your life if you are not loving yourself." The Dai Lai Lama said, "A loving atmosphere in your home is the foundation for your life." I have numerous clients who are blown away with how much more productive they are when they become deliberate about scheduling regular play and nurturing time. Balance is an important trait for success. Everything happens best with balance, including high achievement. In most cases we are rather stingy with ourselves.

Loving yourself also means keeping your word and being in alignment so that your thoughts, words, and actions are all one. Loving yourself includes knowing when to say no to others and honoring your boundaries. This means listening to your inner urges even when no one else seems to agree with you. In short, loving yourself means doing everything in your power to live the greatest life you possibly can.

ACTION STEPS TO LOVE YOURSELF

1. Today, write out five new ways to love yourself and put them in your schedule.

2. Each week make sure you have at least one fun activity that you will do just for yourself where you don't bring anyone along with you.

3. Every day spend at least one hour doing something you love.

#68   Fear

Fear. It is the number one killer of goals, ambitions, ideas, talent, and dreams. It stops us dead in our tracks. It disguises itself in the form of procrastination, worry, oversleeping, laziness, pessimism, cynicism, skepticism, justifying, complaining, blaming, doubt, and disbelief. If we are not fearful of rejection, then we are fearful of looking bad. If we are not fearful of being unworthy, then we are fearful that we don't have it in us to do what it takes to have what we so desire, hence we do nothing.

Since fear is so deadly, so dangerous, so painful, scary, and uncomfortable, how do we get rid of it? How do we make it go away, never to return. The answer is simple, but you may not like it. As Susan Jeffers said, "You must feel the fear and do it anyway." Fear never just totally goes away. It may dissipate, but it will surely come up again with something else. As soon as fear is no longer present in one area of your life, it begins to resurface again the minute you begin to stretch outside of your new comfort zone. Even if it shows up in a new way, the fear will still present itself one way or another. The closest thing to a cure is action. The more action you take, the more the fear subsides, and the less control it has over you and the quicker you move through it. Yet the action needs to be a continual way of being. Moving through the fear is the price you pay in order to tap into your greatness. It is the road you must travel in order to grow yourself so that you are ultimately bigger than any challenge that could come your way. To most people, this is a price that they are not willing to pay, but when you consider the alternative, it is the most rewarding choice. It is not the easiest choice, but it is the best one for your spirit. T. Harv Eker said, "If you learn to do things that are hard then life will become easy. If you only do things that are easy, then life will be hard."

However, fear is not something to be dreaded; it is simply a sign that you are growing. Consequently, moving through the fear is the only way that you can grow. If you did not go through this process you would always remain at your current levels in every area of life. This would destroy the spirit because as mentioned before, your natural state is one of growth. Again, "we are like plants, either you are growing or dying." Yet the conditioned mind hates growth. Its main job is protection and keeping things the exact same way they are. This is not a bad thing because you need to have protection too, but in most cases we get so wrapped up in this very tricky aspect of the mind because it knows exactly how to play on our weaknesses. As T. Harv Eker said, "The conditioned mind knows exactly what to say in order to take you out." In other words, if you have a fear of failure, poverty, looking bad, etc., then the conditioned mind will use these things to create that fear in you. Most people are being run by their conditioned mind and don't even know it. As a result fear paralyzes them and they live unfulfilled lives. The secret to overcoming fear and the conditioned mind is to make peace with it and to be able to recognize when it is holding you back in some way and then to simply make the adjustment necessary by diving right into the heart of whatever is causing the fear in the first place.

ACTION STEPS FOR OVERCOMING FEAR

1. Determine to always embrace your fear instead of running from it.

2. Bypass fear by keeping your word and constantly doing things that create more love, joy, fun, success, self-expression, growth, and greater use of your gifts.

3. As you proceed through your day, whenever you notice fear coming your way, simply let it be, (meaning, don't fight it) then take the action necessary to have what you want and deserve. The fear will understand that it cannot stop you and will go away only to try again another day.

#69 Affirmations

Affirmations. When you have something important to do and you're feeling a bit overwhelmed by it, harness the power of affirmations. An affirmation is a positive statement in the present tense that declares that your desired outcome is already in place. Many people have trouble doing this because they feel like they need to see it to believe it, but as Wayne Dyer said, "You will see it when you believe it." This tool will enhance your ability to believe it. Speaking out loud to yourself as if you are currently accomplishing your goal helps to make you unstoppable.

Affirmations are another way to condition your mind for success. Whether they are called affirmations, incantations, or declarations, they are all pretty much the same thing with a slight variation in how much physical movement and emotion a person includes with them. Regardless of the name used to describe them, it is important to understand that they support you with creating absolute certainty when there is doubt. Now you might be saying, "Well, what if I don't believe what I'm affirming?" Just continue to repeat the affirmation to yourself at least fifty times in a day with tremendous energy. The words will seep into your subconscious and affect your actions even if at first you are not convinced. Eventually your old beliefs will shift and with this new certainty, you will take the appropriate actions and attract what you desire in life. This may sound a bit airy-fairy, but this strategy is proven and has been tested time and time again by masters of success. So model them.

Affirmations work whether a person believes they do or not. When a person says the words "I am strong" repeatedly, even if they don't believe the words, when muscle testing is performed on this individual as they are speaking these words, they demonstrate a stronger response then when they say the words "I am weak." This process is metaphysical, but it is also scientific. Remember we are walking computers. You cannot have good input without eventually having good output.

Affirmations condition the mind as well as raise your energy level. They have you vibrate on the frequency of that which you want. Everything is energy even though you can't see it. The things you desire have energy in them as well. In order for you to attract them in your life, you have to radiate the same energy as those things you desire. In this way you are very much like a magnet. In one of her books, prosperity guru Catherine Ponder mentions how simply saying affirmations for fifteen minutes a day will have a greater benefit than 85 percent of the self-development work that a person could do with other books, seminars, and CDs. This is a very strong statement. Yet I have found it to be quite true.

GUIDELINES FOR USING AFFIRMATIONS

1. Look at what your goals are for the year and state them in the first person, in the positive, and as if they are already so. An example is "I attract tremendous abundance as I now make one hundred thousand dollars" or "I now have amazing health and vitality, weighing a solid 150 pounds."

2. Make sure your affirmations include empowering feelings and emotions as well as the specific measurable result you are after. This way you experience the emotions while you are moving toward your goals. For example, "I now have an amazingly fun, loving, romantic relationship such that I marry my partner in June of this year."

3. Say your affirmations for your goals for the year every day in the first hour of the day for at least fifteen minutes, out loud, with as much energy and enthusiasm as you can muster. Also say affirmations during the day for anything that you are feeling is missing or not where you want it to be. For example, if you feel like you have no time, money, energy, or love, affirm that you have those things. This will enable you to more quickly shift your belief, energy, actions, and, ultimately, your results.

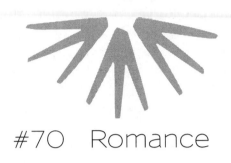

#70   Romance

Romance. What a wonderful thing. When you are involved in romance it can be an absolutely intoxicating feeling, a truly creative expression of love. Yet romance has a few secrets about it, which, if you don't know, can cause tremendous frustration. Whenever you are in love, it is merely the initial phase of a relationship. This initial phase can feel very much like being intoxicated. The other person is perfect in your eyes and can do no wrong. This first phase is how nature basically gives you a head start. In this initial phase, people tend to express their love in a number of romantic ways.

Dr. Gary Chapman wrote an incredible book called *The 5 Love Languages*, in which he describes the five main ways that people experience love. They are words of affirmation, acts of service, quality time, gifts, and touch. We all have a primary and a secondary love language. That means you may enjoy each of these languages, but your primary one is an absolute must in order for you to experience love, with your secondary one being the next strongest need in order for you to feel loved by another person.

In the initial phase of love we tend to hit all five love languages because we are trying to win the other person's affection. In this stage, romance tends to be at an all-time high. This is also the phase of the relationship when we feel like we are walking on a cloud. The thing about this phase is that studies show that it will last around two years at the most. When this wears off, we stop hitting all the love languages and revert to giving love to our partners according to our own love languages. This would be fine, but 80 percent of couples have different love languages. In other words, when a relationship has moved to this second stage, each person can feel like they are not getting what they really need.

This is where the secret of romance comes in. It is imperative that you learn your partner's love languages and become a master in expressing love to them in that particular way consistently. It is the only way they will continually feel emotionally fulfilled in relationship with you. Therefore, the secret to an incredible love relationship is not just being romantic in the beginning but to continually be romantic according to your partner's primary and secondary love languages even after the intoxicating in-love phase is over. If you make this a daily focus, then not only will your partner be thrilled, but they will naturally want to reciprocate and learn to apply your love languages with expressing love to you. This is the way to truly master romance so that it is long lasting.

Action Steps to Master Romance

1. Make a commitment to become a master at romance so that you can continually get better at fulfilling your partner's needs for a lifetime.

2. Learn your partner's love languages by (1) paying attention to what your partner nags you about. This will let you know how you can emotionally please them. (2) Ask your partner when they have felt most loved by you. Their answers will tell you their love languages. (3) Get Gary Chapman's book *The 5 Love Languages* and have both of you take the Love Language self-test.

3. Deliberately plan out what romantic things you are going to do for your significant other each week. Do at least three things. Ideally have one of them be spontaneous, where you ask them what they would like in that moment.

#71 Confidence

Confidence. It is not something that you are simply born with. Yet it is crucial to your success. When someone is confident, they move much more deliberately toward their goals than someone without it. However, many people have a misconception about confidence in that they think that they have to have experience in a particular area before they can have it. As a result of this thinking they do not pursue their dreams because quite often they are in areas where they have no experience. This mind-set will never create confidence. As Tony Robbins said, "If everyone had to already accomplish something in order to have confidence, then nobody would ever have it." You must be able to inject yourself with the confidence before you leap into the unknown. So how do you attain this state of being? One major way is through movement. How you walk and carry yourself affect how you feel. In general, does your posture tend to be slumped over or held up high? Do you speak at a slow, sluggish pace or a more rapid and enthusiastic pace? Do you tend to breathe deep or shallow. The vast majority of the population does not breathe deeply enough to fully energize themselves and be at high levels of health and confidence. People who are confident, walk, talk, dress, and speak in ways that add to their self-esteem. They may not always feel like they can achieve everything they desire, but these practices strengthen their sense of themselves and carry them through the uncertain times. "Motion creates emotion." Always be conscious of how you are using your body.

Confidence must be nurtured. In order to have it, you must live into your vision of your highest self. We all have an ideal way that we would like to handle our lives and create success. Increasing your confidence means you must play that role and live into that vision. If your ideal self-concept is hazy, then clarify it. Similar to an actor in a play or a movie, eventually you will quite naturally become that character. As you go through your day, practice having a smile while walking, thinking, and moving, as if you can accomplish anything. In essence, "fake it till you make it." Before you know it, you will be a confident person.

Action is one of the biggest components to having confidence. In order to be confident, you must act in confident ways. You must take the actions that you would if you already had that confidence. Remember, "you are much more likely to act your way into feeling than to feel your way into acting."

Lastly, it is imperative that you keep your word. This is where a huge amount of your self-esteem comes from. A person's level of success can only be as high as the level of their self-esteem. If you do not keep your word then you will lose respect for yourself as well as trust in your ability to create. On top of that, when you don't keep your word you don't feel worthy or deserving of what you say you want. The flip side to this is that when you live by your word, your confidence just continues to grow over time. Even though fear may still come up, as you consistently keep your word you will develop an unshakable knowing that what you desire or something better is on its way, because you always do what it takes to receive it.

ACTION STEPS TO CREATE CONFIDENCE

1. Physically walk, talk, speak, and dress like you are already the successful person you desire to be.

2. Take the actions that are in total alignment with your goals so you fully position yourself to achieve them.

3. Keep your word. Lovingly honor your commitments to yourself and other people.

#72   Use It or Lose It

Use it or lose it. This is a phrase that is casually used and said often. Yet there is great wisdom in these five words, because they are stating a universal law that can be applied to virtually any scenario. Take your finances, for example. In order to have financial abundance, you need to use your money to make more income for you through investments. If this is not done, there is little chance that you will ever be financially free. With your relationships, you need to constantly nurture them in new and creative ways or else the relationship will fade and become stagnant. With your health and fitness, you must constantly exercise and get the proper nutrition in order for your body to develop or else it will begin to deteriorate. With your career, you must constantly be learning and studying so you can grow and keep up with other leaders in your field. Otherwise, you will get left behind.

With anything that you are working toward, just remember if you are not using it, then you are losing it. We must constantly be growing during our short time on this earth. It is the only way to be totally fulfilled and the only way to continually reach new levels of success and happiness. Again Tony Robbins summed it up this way: "Those who do well with what they have will be given more." Once again it bears repeating that human beings are very much like plants in that you are either growing or dying. Thought of in another light, anything that does not contribute is eliminated.

Again Tony Robbins gave a great perspective on viewing this principle when he said that "you must conduct your life with an emphasis on CANI," which stands for constant and never-ending improvement." The main areas that you want to use CANI with are on the four quadrants of your life. They are health and fitness, finances, relationships, and your career or dream projects. By applying CANI to each quadrant, you ensure that you get the most value out of yourself, and you leave behind a legacy that you can be proud of.

ACTION STEPS TO USE SO YOU DON'T LOSE IT

1. Make a decision to apply constant and never-ending improvement to the four main quadrants of your life, namely, health and fitness, finances, relationships, and your career or dream projects.

2. Become intensely goal-oriented in your achievement and pursuit of goals on a daily, weekly, monthly, and yearly basis so that you naturally grow in all areas.

3. Learn to see every challenge as an opportunity for growth instead of a problem to shy away from. This creates enthusiasm, fun, and greater speed to success.

#73   Thoughts

Thoughts. "Things that make you go hmmmmmmh." Actually they are a lot more than that. Your thoughts determine your destiny. I know that might sound extreme, especially considering that we have so many thoughts that we wish did not enter our consciousness. Yet this does not mean that you can never have a worrisome or fearful thought. You wouldn't be human if you didn't. However, you certainly can control the predominant thoughts and focus of your mind. Remember, human beings can pretty much only focus on one thing at a time. This ability to direct your attention is your greatest ability in life because everything else you create stems from it.

As I have mentioned before, the mind attracts to it whatever it feeds on. Remember the computer analogy, it won't give you good information unless it receives good input. Dr. Lee Pulos, PhD, states in his audio, *How to Recondition Your Mind for Automatic Success*, that the average person has forty-five to fifty thousand thoughts a day. Dr. Pulos states that the overwhelming majority of these thoughts are negative. Dr. Pulos also cites a study where the thoughts of so-called average people were monitored, and they recorded around thirty positive thoughts to every four hundred or so negative ones. This kind of statistic is staggering when you consider that 80 percent of your success depends on how you are mentally, emotionally, and spiritually. The other 20 percent is based on which actions you take.

This is why conditioning the mind to have positive, empowering thoughts is absolutely critical to your success. In this way you strengthen your subconscious mind. It has been said that "worry is the misuse of imagination." The subconscious affects the conscious mind by telling it what to do. The subconscious mind does not care whether its thoughts are negative or positive. Its job is simply to follow the messages and commands it is given whether you are aware of them or not. The way to ensure that your subconscious gives the right messages to you is to make sure that your thoughts focus on what you want in your life. Again, there will be times when you have thoughts that are so way out that you will wonder where they came from, but it is in these moments that you need to gently bring your attention right back to the peaceful, loving abundance that you wish to manifest in your life. "You become what you think about most of the time."

Action Steps to Have Great Thoughts

1. Today and every day practice the art of focused attention. Napoleon Hill said, "Spend so much time focusing on what you want that you don't have time to think about what you don't want."

2. Use tools such as visualization, affirmation, meditation, and prayer on a daily basis for at least an hour in the morning.

3. Strengthen the mind by constantly feeding it self-development books, audios, and courses so that you continue to expand your knowledge and, therefore, your thoughts.

#74   Procrastination

Procrastination. It's been called the silent killer and the thief of time. No matter how talented or intelligent you are, if procrastination consistently overtakes you, then you may as well throw in the towel on realizing your intentions. Everyone procrastinates from time to time, but you must be aware of when it is starting to take effect. If you are unconscious of when you are procrastinating then you could end up attributing your results to other circumstances instead of taking full responsibility for your procrastination.

There are a number of ways that procrastination takes people out, but many of these ways are not seen as procrastination at all by most people. Instead they are simply seen as life. Sometimes when you feel sleepy, it means procrastination is trying to creep in. Often times sleep is merely resistance to doing what needs to be done to move you forward. Bear in mind that "nothing is more draining of your energy than having unfinished tasks that need to be completed," as Steve Chandler said. Procrastination can also show up when you are easily distracted from what you are doing. For example, if you have a project to complete for work and you constantly allow such interruptions as the telephone or e-mails to distract you, then you are procrastinating. Many people will say that they are just putting out fires that need to be taken care of, but this is ultimately a lack of focus and follow-through on what is most important. Instead of reacting to every distraction, have a set time where you only respond to e-mails and phone calls. The most effective people schedule chunks of time to do these things. Granted, some demands truly do warrant immediate responses but far less than most people admit. Successful people are clear about what is absolutely most important, and they only get involved with lesser tasks after their priorities have been taken care of.

Some other possible ways that you can be procrastinating are when you are creating unnecessary drama in your life or when you are increasingly disinterested, irritable, blaming others, constantly confused, refusing help, complaining, and are disengaging from people or things that support your progress. Any of these situations should serve as a signal to refocus your energy and attention on what is most important in your life.

ACTION STEPS FOR OVERCOMING PROCRASTINATION

1. Do the most difficult and most important tasks earlier in the day instead of later. The later you wait, the harder they become to do.

2. If a task is constantly getting put off but needs to be done, then just make a scheduled appointment to work on it for five minutes. After the five minutes you can do something else, but giving this amount of time is something the mind can digest, and usually once you get into it, you may do even more than five minutes.

3. Remember the 80/20 rule. Only 20 percent of what you do gets you to where you want to be. Successful people spend at least 50 percent of their time in the zone. This means work to spend at least half of your time only focusing on 20 percent tasks. You can determine a 20 percent task with regards to your goals because "they are harder, take longer, and tend to involve more risks," as Robert Allen said.

#75 Momentum

Momentum. Ooooooohhhhh, it is a beautiful thing. It is a powerful invisible energy that if nurtured properly can carry you to all your dreams and beyond. The funny thing about success is that most people actually already have some idea of what actions need to be taken to begin to move in the direction of their goals, but they just don't know how to begin, continue, or to complete what they have started.

Let's take something basic like health and fitness. If someone wants to be a certain weight, then the chances are very high that they know that eating right and exercise are keys to hitting their goal. However, due to fear of failure, success, the unknown, or simply not having a strong-enough sense of self, the person will not move forward. The wonderful thing about momentum is that if a person can just have enough courage to take the first step, and then the next, and continue to only focus on the next one step at a time, even if they don't have all the answers, then eventually they will have created so much power behind their intention that nothing will be able to stop them, not even themselves. Doubts will still come up, as will fear, but the momentum will be so strong that even when the person gets off course, they will find themselves continuing to move forward. Ambrose Redmoon said, "Courage is not the absence of fear, but rather the judgment that something else is more important than fear." To a large extent this is basic physics. "An object in motion will tend to stay in motion, while an object at rest will tend to stay at rest." Similar to a snowball rolling down a hill or a locomotive that reaches its top speed, it is almost impossible to stop someone with a great deal of momentum.

This process does not happen all at once, but it gets stronger with every single action you take. Once you have established a track record of taking productive steps toward a particular outcome, then you will be much more apt to follow through during those times when you don't feel like it, simply because you won't want to mess up the momentum. As Brian Tracy said, "Nothing is more motivating than success." In this way you become like a freight train, such that the speed you have already generated is carrying you, and it is harder for obstacles to impede your progress. Hence, your success will breed more success.

Action Steps to Create Unstoppable Momentum

1. Look to do something every day to move you toward your most important goals.

2. Make sure you consistently eat right, exercise, get proper rest, play great music, and are organized so that you have the energy to keep your commitments.

3. Create a solid spiritual routine by using the power tools of meditation, journaling, affirming, and visualizing every day.

#76 Choice

Choice. The freedom of choice is a big issue for most, yet rarely do we exercise it to the max. Every single thing you do is a choice, from getting up in the morning and brushing your teeth, to going to work and staying involved in your current relationships. Instead of feeling like life is a burden and you have to do something, focus on how you get to choose everything you do. Now you might be saying, "But I have to pay my mortgage and go to work." Not if you don't want to. Of course there are consequences that go along with those decisions, but you are choosing a certain outcome by going to work. In the same light you may also decide that you are going to choose a new kind of work for yourself. If you continue to work your old job while creating or finding a new one, you are still choosing.

When you are approaching each decision from a place of choice, you stand in your power. By doing this you take full responsibility for your life and ownership of the moments that you create each day. It is impossible to take this stand and be a victim. Victims constantly blame and complain about the circumstances of their life. Whenever you are doing this you are denying your power because it takes away a sense of your ability to create your own reality.

When you have the awareness that you are choosing something instead of it just happening to you, you are liberated. This gives you a sense of freedom because you understand that your choices create your outcomes. You are no longer putting more stock in outside world circumstances than you are in your own power to create. Even if you are doing something that you feel is challenging in order to get to a more desirable place, be clear that you are deciding to do that. While you are doing it, ask yourself an empowering question like "How can I do it and have fun?" In this way you are choosing to do a difficult activity and to turn it into a fun one all because of your mind-set.

You have so much input into your life. Remember that your life right now is the result of every choice you have made in the past with your thoughts and actions. Channel this power and enjoy the process by being conscious of every single choice you make. This is the empowering way to shape your destiny; besides, it feels so much better.

ACTION STEPS FOR MAKING A GREAT CHOICE

1. Always make your decisions with long-term perspective. Think of how this decision will affect your goals for the day, week, month, year, etc.

2. Anytime you need to make a decision, come up with at least three possible options so that you have a range of choices. If you are trying to decide between two things that you want, ask yourself the millionaire question, which is "How can I have both?" "Rich people always think both," as T. Harv Eker said.

3. When trying to make the right choice, also ask yourself the question "How will I feel about myself afterward if I go with this particular option?" The best choice will always have you feel good about yourself.

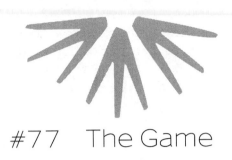

#77　The Game

The game. Human beings love games. They stimulate us mentally, nourish us emotionally, and sometimes challenge us physically. If a person is invited to play a game, typically they will jump at the opportunity, be it for a sport, video, mental, or board game. Yet when a so-called problem arises in our life, we moan and groan. This is merely a matter of perspective. "Remember that 80 percent of your success in life depends on how you are mentally, emotionally, and spiritually." Tony Robbins said "you can put two people in an identical situation with all of the same problems, and one person can totally rise above it to great success while the other person goes on a downward spiral and hits rock bottom." The main thing that determines which direction a person will go depends on their mind-set and attitude. Successful people have extremely optimistic outlooks in even the most challenging situations. They expect to be a success even if it takes them a while and see everything as ultimately leading them closer to success. Instead of seeing life's obstacles as burdens, see them as parts of the game.

When you think about it, life is the greatest game of all time. By simply shifting your lens and seeing your so-called problems as opportunities, you will become like a star athlete who takes challenges and turns them into big breakthroughs. Marianne Williamson said, "Our worst fear is not that we are inadequate, our deepest fear is that we are powerful beyond measure. It is our light not our darkness that most frightens us. We ask ourselves who am I to be brilliant, talented, gorgeous and fabulous? Actually who are you not to be? You are a child of God." There is a star athlete in all of us, and it is bigger than any obstacle. When you embrace this inner athlete, you not only reach great heights in your life, but you also enjoy the ride much more. Williamson goes even deeper with this concept when she says "You're playing small doesn't serve the world. There is nothing enlightened about shrinking so that other people won't feel insecure around you. We were born to make manifest the glory of God within us. It is not just in some of us, it is in everyone and as we let our own light shine we unconsciously give other people permission to do the same. As we are liberated from our own fear, our presence automatically liberates others." You must remember that with each goal, it is the process that must also be enjoyed and not just the final destination, because quite often the high of reaching your end result can be short-lived. Therefore, you must use empowering perspectives and appreciate every step of the way. So from this day forward, with every obstacle, think about how you would go about solving the problem if you were to approach it as if it were part of a game. With this mind-set you will draw on more of your inner resources, and pretty soon you will begin to see yourself as a winner in the game.

ACTION STEPS TO WIN THE GAME

1. With every problem, decide to call it a challenge and ask yourself what piece of the puzzle you need to provide in order to win the game.

2. Use rewards for each difficult step that you need to take in order to acknowledge your progress and to make the game more fun as you advance to the next level.

3. In the immortal words of Wayne Dyer, "Don't take yourself so damn seriously." Lighten up. The lighter you are, the more you can flow with and through each situation.

#78 Failure

Failure. What a word. For most people this term is fully loaded. The weight it carries is so heavy that it stops people in their tracks. Fear of failure kills countless dreams, ideas, and aspirations. One might ask if the fear of failure is so detrimental, why does the vast majority of the human population get stuck because of it? The reason is that they associate more pain to the possibility of failure than they do the pleasure of surpassing it. The mere thought of rejection, looking bad, or moving beyond one's comfort zone is just too much to bear. Most people take failure as a personal statement about their own self-worth. Studies show that two-thirds of people have low self-esteem.

If a person already has low self-esteem, they are going to be even more sensitive to something that their mind could use to confirm that they are not good enough. In this way the failure ends up being a self-fulfilling prophecy. Regardless of the endeavor, the failure ends up serving as a validation for the person's worst fear of all, which is simply that they are not worthy or good enough. Because of this dynamic, the average person quits at something after trying less than one time. Failure ends up being something that most people will avoid like a plague. The average person wants to simply keep things the exact way they are so they are not in danger of failing. The problem with this is that it prevents you from being in your natural state of growth and has you live a lukewarm life. Remember the saying "use it or lose it." We are put on this planet and given this life to continually grow, expand,

and use our gifts to serve ourselves and humanity. This requires that we constantly grow. So if a person is always avoiding anything that would have them fail, then they may be safe, but they will never ever be truly happy and self-expressed because they are not in their natural state of being. As a result they will lose their special gifts and talents because they will never be developed.

A person who is an achiever, on the other hand, looks at failure from a very different perspective. They give it an entirely different meaning. Miles Davis said, "Do not fear mistakes, there are none." The successful person sees failure as a stepping stone, a learning experience, an advancement that has now placed the odds increasingly in their favor. Before Thomas Edison created the lightbulb, he failed more than ten thousand times. Initially people thought he was crazy to attempt such a thing in the first place. After his invention was completed and he was asked why he didn't ever quit, his response was, "I had to succeed because finally I just ran out of things that didn't work." If you could shift your sense of thinking and take on the perspective of the achiever when you fail, then you could push through and experience a fulfillment and greatness that is beyond anything you could imagine. You must never give up. The people who are the greatest successes are quite often those who have failed the most. Henry Ford's words bear repeating when he said that "failure is just an opportunity to start over again more intelligently."

Action Steps to Use Failure

1. Make it a habit anytime you have a failure to simply ask what's next, in order to move forward, and then act immediately in some capacity on the answer.

2. Every time you fail look to see how the feedback you got from the failure can be used to move you forward on your goal.

3. Constantly remind yourself that some failure is natural and necessary to be a great success at anything.

#79   Reflections

Reflections. Have you ever considered how your outer world is simply a reflection and manifestation of your inner world? Most people never examine this. They feel that their life experience is a matter of chance, the luck of the draw, or due to some external set of circumstances. Yet what you cannot see creates what you can see. In other words, you manifest your life. The laws of cause and effect are always at work. As an example, let's examine the realm of money. Let's say someone is not happy with how much they make. The majority of the time they will blame that result on the economy, their boss, or some other outside influence. What they are not considering is that money along with many other outcomes is merely a result. It is a result of not only one's actions, but also one's thoughts and beliefs as well.

T. Harv Eker has a saying: "If you want to understand the fruits on your tree, you must examine the roots." Most experiences end up playing out as situations that reflect a person's core beliefs. On the surface, you may say that you believe one thing, but you can always tell what your predominant beliefs are because they are directly reflected in your results. Now you may say that you do believe that you can have money, success, or happiness, but you just always seem to have bad breaks. If this is the case then you have mixed associations, and so you are getting mixed results.

The universe is constantly giving you feedback that lets you know how you need to adjust in order to attract your intention. If, for example, you are in a relationship with someone that is not paying you very much attention, then that reflection is very valuable feedback that is letting you know that in some way, shape, or form you need to give yourself more love and attention. If the person is not giving you the kind of respect that you want, then you need to respect yourself more. This may be by taking a stand in the relationship or simply respecting the guidance of your intuition instead of second-guessing it. When you learn to view reflections as signs from the universe about how you need to shift internally and externally, you are harnessing your power to shape your world.

ACTION STEPS FOR USING REFLECTIONS

1. Always remember that you are extremely powerful, and create your life by attracting everything into it with your thoughts and beliefs.

2. If you find you don't like a certain result in your life, ask yourself how you can use that reflection to make the proper internal and external changes to move past the obstacle and forward to your goal. As Einstein said, "You can't solve a problem with the same mind that created it."

3. With every situation, make sure to focus on your intention with love and gratitude while taking the perfect actions to put it in place. In this way, you will have the greatest reflections.

#80 Now

Now. Have you ever just sat and pondered about how all you really have in your life is now? Regardless of what you have accomplished, or failed at in the past, and despite whatever your intentions are for the future, your life equals the present moment. Nothing has more meaning or power than what you do with these precious seconds that are now in your hands. They are a microcosm of your entire existence. They can strengthen or weaken your legacy. It simply depends on how you decide to use your time right now. When you realize that each minute is all you have to write your own personal success story, it suddenly becomes a lot easier to be present in where you are now. This is also the greatest way to forward your mission.

Most people are so busy scurrying that they are not fully present in what they are engaged in at that moment. Their mind is normally somewhere else, or at least partially. They are either living in the past by dragging old experiences and ways of thinking to each new situation, or they are so focused on the future big picture that they are not being fully engaged in the now. Both of these ways of being have limiting setbacks. When you are bringing old baggage to the present moment you are coloring the experience such that you are not able to see possibility and create the moment from a new and fresh perspective. Instead, everything is just being viewed as another version of your past. In other words, living this way severely limits your growth. Yet the other extreme of living in the future can be problematic as well, because you can miss the details of today. Having a vision for the future is empowering, but if a person misses taking care of all the important details of today then their future vision won't be able to materialize. Whereas when you do what needs to be done now then your future vision will take care of itself.

The key to fully embracing the now, as it is with everything else, is balance. On the one hand, you need to be open to what is showing up in the moment and go with the flow based on your intentions. On the other hand, you need to be clear about your goals for the future and make sure you act now on the details that need to be handled in order to get you there. When you are able to do this dance, you fully enjoy each moment and accomplish your goals. Now is ultimately what determines your destiny. As the saying goes, "yesterday is history, tomorrow is a mystery, today is a gift. That is why it is called present."

ACTION STEPS FOR LIVING IN THE NOW

1. Forget your past. Even forget your future for the moment, and become fully present to now. Take a second to really just absorb and appreciate everything that is happening around you. The more you can fully live in the now, the greater your life will become.

2. Live into your intention for each moment by envisioning your perfect day before it starts and simply reaffirming it anytime you feel you are off course.

3. Have a clear vision with goals for the future that are written down. Make sure you act now on the critical details that must be taken care of in order for you to get to where you want to be. As the incredible W. Clement Stone said with his most famous affirmation, "Do it now."

#81 Truth

Truth. What a noble, grandiose word. The truth is the essence, the foundation, the very stuff that dreams are made of. Why? Why is the truth so vital? It is because without it you cannot experience your highest self. One must move beyond the stories and negative self chatter of the ego in order to experience the oneness of the self. This process means being able to decipher the truth through the different forms of resistance that present themselves in our daily lives. Tony Robbins said, "You cannot lie to yourself and expect the truth to be a part of your life." Once again, "the only thing that keeps you from having all that you desire are your stories and reasons about why you can't have it."

Most people's stories and excuses are much bigger than their desire to take responsibility for the results they are getting. There are many reasons for this, but the biggest one always comes back to fear. Everything that human beings do is in some way or another to meet their needs. Tony Robbins explains that we have six human needs. The first one is the need for certainty. We all have a need to feel certain about our safety and certain about having some control over our lives. The second need is the need for uncertainty or variety. We all have a need for a certain amount of variety in our lives. The third need is the need for significance. We all have a need to feel important and like we make a difference. The fourth need is the need for love and connection. The first four needs are needs of the personality.

This means that human beings will absolutely do whatever it takes to meet these needs. The last two needs are called needs of the spirit because they are more spiritual in nature. The fifth need is the need for growth, and the sixth need is the need for contribution.

These needs are significant to understand because whenever a person is consistently having problems, in some way or the other they are creating them in their life because they are simply trying to meet one or more of their needs. With problems it is normally one of the first four needs that a person is trying to fulfill. Even though the person is doing it in an entirely disempowering way, they are still just trying to get their needs met. For example, if a person is always cursing out other people, they most likely are looking to meet the need of significance because they are trying to feel important. Even though this is not a very effective strategy, it is meeting the need. The tricky thing about human needs is that most people will often go about meeting them in disempowering ways; to meet them in empowering ways means that they would have to confront their fears and be, have, and do more to move through them. For most people this is too scary so they take the easy and unfulfilling route by creating certain problems and being a victim in some way. As T. Harv Eker put it, "You either have reasons or results." We must be brutally honest with ourselves and realize when our interpretations are skewed or selling us short. This is hard. This is humbling. This is the truth.

ACTION STEPS FOR LIVING BY THE TRUTH

1. Take full responsibility for every area of your life.

2. With each personal situation, ask yourself "How did I set it up?"

3. When you have a problem, ask yourself "What needs am I meeting and how else could I meet them in an empowering way?"

#82   Feelings

Feelings. We are socialized in such a way that does not allow us to regard our feelings. Most of us simply just do not know how to deal with them. We run away from them, suppress them, get mad or embarrassed that we have them, or try to stop ourselves from feeling them all together. We are taught that it is not nice to have feelings of anger, guilt, jealously, or sorrow. Only cheerful emotions are seen as okay. Men are told don't cry, women are told to always be nice. Whereas the uncomfortable emotions are less easy to be with, they are no less significant.

As John Gray put it, "Feelings are little messengers, and they will keep knocking on the door until we get the message." All feelings must be acknowledged. It does not mean that you cannot shift your state or outlook, but you must first admit what action the feeling is leading you to. For example, feelings of hurt or anger may mean that you need to communicate these emotions to someone and then perform a loving act for yourself. A feeling of guilt may mean that you have violated one of your most important standards. Feelings of jealousy may mean that you need to get back in touch with a forgotten dream or aspiration that you once had.

The one huge taboo that must be avoided at all costs is trying to stop a feeling from coming up because "the more you resist, the more it persists." Your feelings are the ultimate guidance system. They let you know what shifts need to be made if any at all. Of course you ideally want to always be feeling good. After all, this is your natural state of being and the way that you feel when you are connected to your source. When you feel good, it is when you are most magnetic to receive abundance and blessings. The reason for this is because all that you desire has feelings of joy associated with it. So in order for you to attract it into your life, you need to radiate those feelings. However, it is unrealistic to think that you are going to feel good every single moment of your life. Therefore, when you notice that you are having any painful emotions, use them to gauge how you need to either change your perspective on the matter, change the actions you are taking, or both. This will immediately shift your energy and put you back on the road to feeling good again.

So honor your feelings, all of them, even the ugly ones. Let it not only be okay to have them, but listen to the message they give you, see the direction they are pointing you in, and go there. Most people don't do this, but then again most people aren't totally self-empowered either.

ACTION STEPS FOR DEALING WITH FEELINGS

1. Always be totally honest while paying close attention to what your feelings are.

2. Have total unconditional acceptance for the feelings no matter how uncomfortable they may be.

3. Let the feelings guide you with how you need to shift your mind-set or actions in order to move through the situation with success and joy.

#83   Peace

Peace. Consider all that you do. All your hopes, dreams, aspirations, goals, fears, failures, and heartaches, in some way or another, stem from the underlying desire to know peace. When you think about it, all your spirit ultimately wants is peace. You may say, "Well, I just want a lot of money or for my children to act a certain way." Yet if examined more closely, you would see that you crave those results because of the feelings you anticipate will accompany them. Whether these feelings are joy, satisfaction, comfort, or security, they all tie in to experiencing peace.

Knowing that this is the spirit's ultimate goal enables you to choose your path accordingly. Peace is what allows you to do your life's work. We all were put on the planet to share our unique gifts in service to humanity. When you are not using those gifts you are blocking your own flow. As a result, you will experience much angst and frustration. You will feel out of sorts and unfulfilled. It will be harder to get along with people. Your health and energy will be lower and you will constantly feel like something is missing. Yet when you are at peace, everything in your life just feels like it is supporting you, and you are able to do what you were born to do.

Living a life of peace ultimately means making choices that are in alignment with your intuition and making choices that enable you to experience the vast reservoir of love within. Remember your intuition is your inner guide. It is your great connection to spirit. It always knows what is the perfect next step to take in any situation. As the saying goes, "spirit speaks to us through our intuition, and we give back to spirit by following that intuition." When you do this, not only are you fully self-expressed, but you are also able to live lovingly. Love is the most powerful force in the universe. It can move mountains. However, to experience this kind of existence means that you must deliberately choose to be an agent of peace and give up your need to fight and be right.

As Wayne Dyer said, "Choose the path of least resistance." This doesn't mean ignore your challenges. It means let love steer the wheel of your life and guide all of your decisions. For example, when you have a choice between showing how right you are about something or simply loving unconditionally, choose love. When you have the option of revenge or release, opt for release. When you can select between tricking or truth, take truth. All of these decisions will lead to peace, and for the one who lives in peace, life flows like cool water on a hot day, easing the tension of the surrounding heat.

Action Steps for Being at Peace

1. Determine to be an agent of peace.

2. Whenever you are faced with a challenging decision or lower energy feelings of anger, guilt, shame, blame, etc., choose the path that will restore you to feelings of peace.

3. Listen to your intuition with everything you do, and let love filter through your entire being, recognizing that it is the greatest power there is.

#84 Meditation

Meditation. Why is it imperative? In a nutshell it will give you your life, not the struggling existence that most people have, but the capacity for the life of your dreams. The successful application of the tools and concepts in this book depend on your inner ability to apply them. This means that you have to expand internally in order to expand externally. One of the greatest ways to do this is through meditation. There are so many different forms of meditation that the number of options is too great to focus on in this passage. The point is not necessarily which form you partake in but, more importantly, that you are doing it.

Meditation is a tool that has been around for thousands of years. Its rewards produce countless benefits and miracles. Meditation connects you to the infinite source that resides within you and is the foundation for the courage and wisdom to live as your highest self. It is a means for being centered while staying lighthearted. It cuts off the constant babble of the mind and the incessant chatter of the ego. This tool also creates spontaneous motivation in one's life. In other words, when you know what you need to do to get to where you want to be but you just can't seem to get yourself going, this is the perfect tool. After sitting down to meditate for five minutes or so, quite often you will find that you now spontaneously want to do what you previously didn't want to. This process also strengthens your ability to focus. By engaging in this practice where you are focusing on your breath and sometimes a mantra, you are strengthening your ability to concentrate. Even though other thoughts may come up, after a while you will be able to hold your attention for longer periods of time without interruption. This same ability to concentrate will carry over to your day-to-day activities, making you far more productive and less easily distracted.

Meditation also offsets negative energy and will clean up many potentially negative experiences that you would otherwise have to go through. When you meditate, not only do you make yourself more positive, but other people as well. Around the year 2000, when Washington DC had the highest crime rate in the United States, there was an experiment done with at least a thousand volunteers for over a month. The volunteers simply meditated on peace in Washington DC, and the result was that the crime rate went down 25 percent. Meditation increases your health and wellness. People who meditate regularly tend to have better blood pressure and circulation. They also tend to be more calm because they have released many emotions that would have otherwise remained stuck and unexpressed. Meditation will also make you more magnetic to receive blessings, because you will be raising your frequency and vibration every time you do it. Again the law of attraction is at work here. The benefits from this discipline are endless. Simply put, this is the most powerful power tool.

ACTION STEPS FOR MEDITATION

1. Experiment with meditating every day for at least ten minutes; if you do not feel that your life has improved after a year, then give it up. As you do this, pay very close attention to the empowering shifts with your mental and emotional states as well as an increase in positive occurrences in your daily experience. They will seem like coincidences, but they are directly related to your inner work.

2. Make sure you meditate as soon as you get out of bed and then visualize ten minutes, write in your journal

twenty minutes, and affirm ten minutes to complete your morning power tools.

3. Make meditation an absolute priority and gradually lengthen this daily practice to an hour a day. This hour can be broken up into two or three segments of morning, noon, and night. Understand that the longer you meditate, the better life gets and the faster it gets there.

#85   Knowledge

Knowledge. Most people think that knowledge is power. It is understandable how someone could feel this way. All great achievements have been realized as a result of someone who has applied knowledge. Yet there is an operative word here that needs to be examined and that is "applied." It is assumed that knowledge automatically equals power. Yet how many people know exactly what they need to do in order to achieve a measured result and still never apply the information they have.

There is an instant comfort zone that people hit when they have attained information. For example, studies show that less than 10 percent of people who buy a book or audio recording will ever finish them. This statistic is staggering when you think about it. The rationale that most people use is that because they have taken action with purchasing the information, they are now comfortable because they have at least done something.

However, as obvious as this misconception can seem, there is another one that is just as tricky, and that is when someone actually takes the time to get educated but does not use the information. This is when a person fully reads the book, completes the course, or listens to the entire audio program but then does not use what they have learned. It is almost as if they feel like the knowledge has guaranteed them the desired outcome, and because they now know how to do it they can relax because the rest is as good as done.

This way of thinking is deceptive because it prevents you from using what you know. It tricks you into being passive. It is the equivalent to having that brand new fully loaded Porsche in your garage and never driving it. The mere thought of this seems absurd, even comical, but this is exactly what many people do. Again it bears repeating that the conditioned mind hates growth and will try to protect you by keeping things the exact same way they are. It is extremely slick and "every time you grow and expand, so does it." Therefore, in a situation where you have just acquired new knowledge but a little voice is telling you that you don't need to apply it now, understand that there are other forces at work. This is just another version of the conditioned mind trying to take you out. You must be crystal clear about the need to work both parts of this formula, and they are knowledge plus application equals power. Leave out any part of this and you leave your dreams right in the garage.

ACTION STEPS FOR USING KNOWLEDGE

1. When you learn something new, immediately look to see some way to apply it. Use a personal coach for support and to keep you accountable.

2. See if you can create a system to incorporate the information in your life. If possible, do it daily. It takes thirty days to create a new habit.

3. If you are learning a lot of different things at once, prioritize and work on one new thing at a time so as to avoid overwhelm.

#86 Teamwork

Teamwork. It is not something that people often equate with tremendous success. Instead we are socialized to be better than everyone else. We are often taught that we must step on one another in order to get ahead. If someone has a lot, many times we take on the mistaken perspective that it means less for us. The truth is not only is there plenty of room at the top, but the best way to arrive there is through cooperation as opposed to competition. The only person we ever need to really compete with is ourselves, and that is simply to go further than we have in the past. Otherwise, it is much more effective to use the minds, capital, and various resources of others to reach great heights.

If you were to study the history of any great successes you would discover that a team of people were collectively responsible for the result and not just one person. Even if it seems like the one person is solely responsible and getting what appears to be all the glory, there are numerous other vital pieces of the puzzle that you may not be able to see. For every great athlete, there is a great coach; every amazing entertainer, a strong manager or agent; for every great business, there are keen advisors, mentors, and board members. We all need people who support our vision and have strengths in areas where we are lacking.

Napoleon Hill referred to this as the mastermind principle. He described it as "the coordination of effort between two or more people in a spirit of perfect harmony in order to attain a specific objective." The reason this concept is so powerful is because by continually working together in a spirit of harmony, you experience greater levels of enthusiasm, faith, action, and courage than would be present if you were to attempt to accomplish the goal by yourself.

Teamwork doesn't mean that you don't take full responsibility for your life. You will still need to do this, but you do it from a place of abundance and understanding that there is more than enough for everyone, and by working with the right people you will more rapidly get to where you want to be. Remember the sayings "no man is an island" and "behind every great man is a great woman." We all need help and support no matter how smart, talented, or determined we are. So begin assembling your special support team today.

ACTION STEPS FOR CREATING GREAT TEAMWORK

1. Hire a life coach. This is extremely important. Not only will you expand as a result of the accountability, but the objective suggestions will prove invaluable. Your team will ultimately be a number of people, but this is a great place to start.

2. Make sure to define what the specific purpose and outcomes are for the team.

3. Be clear about the plan to reach the outcome as well as what each person's role is and what benefit they will receive as a result of their participation.

#87   Problem Solving

Problem solving. No matter how great your life is, you will still have problems. Even if you take on a powerful mind-set and choose to call these problems challenges, they are no less present. Even if you have the wisdom to see the gems hidden in the triumph over each problem, the issues themselves are no less pressing. You still have to face them in order to experience total peace of mind.

It has been said countless times that "success leaves clues." Part of being successful is engaging in the study of success. One of the strongest patterns of successful people is that they tend to be great problem solvers. Unsuccessful people tend to dwell on the hardship of their problems and play the role of the victim. Successful people search tirelessly for solutions, and because you get what you focus on, successful people tend to get the answers to solve their problems.

The ability to problem solve is a tremendous asset. It will not only make it easier to navigate through challenging situations, but you will also be able to provide even more value. The greatest entrepreneurs are actually the greatest problem solvers. They provide a service or product that in some way or another provides value. If this value were not present, the consumer's life would be more problematic. So in essence, the greatest entrepreneurs solve the greatest number of problems for the greatest number of people.

Problem solving also enables you to grow and become a far more resourceful person. T Harv Eker said, "It's never the size of the problem that's the issue, it's only the size of you." If you have a level-5 problem but you are a level-2 person, then it is the end of the world; but if you have a level-5 problem and you are a level-10 person, it's just a small challenge. Therefore, "it is pivotal that you continually grow yourself so that you are bigger than any problem," as Harv said. Since you are virtually guaranteed that different problems/challenges will present themselves for the rest of your life, this is a worthwhile skill to attain.

Action Steps for Problem Solving

1. Determine to be a great problem solver. Whenever a problem arises, embrace the challenge and see it as an opportunity to grow your problem-solving muscle.

2. Plan out the solution. Get clear on the end result. Write it down. Give it a deadline. Note all the steps. Prioritize the steps. Schedule the steps, and take action every day until the goal is attained and the problem is solved.

3. Go within. Whenever one of these so-called challenges decides to rear its head, this is a time to meditate and pray. Nothing will give a person better or quicker access to their highest wisdom than the use of these tools. Through them the path to the best solution will be revealed. Let all problems, whether big or small, be an action signal to get in touch with your inner guidance. It will always let you know what the next best step is. Simply continue to meditate on the answer until you have clarity about it. As Wayne Dyer's said, "There is a spiritual solution to every problem."

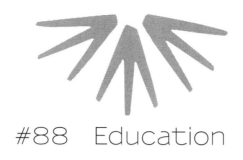

#88 Education

Education. It is generally agreed upon that college is expected to be a part of a person's educational agenda. The mainstream thinking says that if you are fortunate enough to have the financial means, then you should go to college. This is what most people have been socialized to believe. Higher education can be a wonderful choice. I am by no means knocking it. In fact, I encourage it. However, once school is over, most people reach a plateau. The emphasis on learning dramatically decreases after school. The focus then becomes primarily about maintaining a person's lifestyle and taking care of their family. Of course these goals are significant as well, but the problem with this thinking is that it disregards the principle that balance is the key to an exceptional life.

By ignoring our need to continually learn and be educated even after college, we are denying a critical component of our core makeup, and that is growth. Growth is an integral part of a person's natural state of being. The spirit literally yearns for it. This is why people feel out of sorts when they are not expanding. The need to grow through education does not cease when school is over, or at any age for that matter. It is a lifelong process. The moment we stop growing, life loses its juice. Again recall those often-used sayings "use it or lose it" or "you are either growing or dying." We really are much like plants. In the same way that they require water to thrive, we require education for personal growth.

Again it is also important to take note of the patterns of extremely successful people. They tend to always be studying. In Brian Tracy's book *The 21 Secrets of Millionaires*, one of the secrets that he notes is that millionaires are lifelong learners. They are always reading, taking courses, and listening to audio programs. This is so important because one piece of information can double or triple your results. It is also significant because information is changing so rapidly that "if you are not getting better, you are getting worse." Today's knowledge is becoming obsolete so fast that if you do not move with the times, you can easily get left behind.

It is also important to note that learning does not necessarily require that you attend a university. Any of the following forms can be just as valuable. Reading, audio listening, and seminars by themselves can not only put you into the top 10 percent in your field, but can also give you secrets for a greater quality of life in all areas. It is important to not only become an expert in your field, but also in relationships, health, and money. These are the main categories of life that have the biggest impact on your happiness and well-being. We are holistic beings, and any part of the whole that is denied will create a ripple effect in the other areas. The greater the level of balance you maintain, the higher the level of harmony and abundance you will experience.

ACTION STEPS FOR EDUCATION

1. Resolve to become a lifelong learner by reading in your field every day for thirty to sixty minutes and continually putting yourself in new learning situations.

2. Take every course in your field that you can.

3. Listen to audio programs on self-development every time you walk, drive, or travel anywhere. On average, your travel time is the equivalent of one or two college semesters per year. Use this time to learn.

#89   Rewards

Rewards. These are wonderful tools for personal success that quite often get overlooked. Normally a reward is thought of as the gold at the end of the rainbow or the cheese at the end of the tunnel. In other words, it is something you are entitled to as you reach the culmination of a long journey. Surely there is tremendous value in this. It is always great to celebrate. The question is what is going on during the journey?

Rewards need to be present throughout the whole process, not just at the end of the road when everything is said and done. So many people struggle with starting projects and continuing to plug through once they have begun them. This is where rewards can really support a person and push them over the top. When you are stuck and having difficulty following through, pick a small treat that you can give yourself for taking the step—a bouquet of flowers, watching a favorite movie, or even a favorite dessert are all great options. It does not have to be something that requires money as long as it is something that acknowledges your progress and brings you joy.

Rewards do three main things that increase your ability to realize goals. The first one is that they acknowledge your progress. So many things that people accomplish go unrecognized by others. Because other people do not give them credit, a person will tend to not give themselves credit either. As a result of this, the person will have trouble identifying themselves as successful. Yet when the habit of rewarding is in place, it becomes much more natural to see yourself as a successful person. This is important because success breeds more success.

The second thing that rewards do is they reinforce the new habits you are looking to put in place. Your level of success is determined by your habits. When you get a prize after a certain behavior it creates a positive association to that behavior, therefore making it easier to form a new habit.

The third extremely powerful benefit of rewards is that they simply make the process of achievement more fun. This tool will not only invoke more motivation but will make the ride that much more enjoyable. Again human beings are motivated by pain and pleasure. Most people are simply not willing to pay the price for the success they seek because they associate too much pain to the amount of work involved. Rewards give the work more of a feeling of play. Instead of the work feeling like such a burden, it becomes like a game where you are aiming for the immediate prize. Consistently using rewards will get you to your goal two to three times faster than without them. You simply have nothing to lose and everything to gain.

Action Steps for Rewards

1. Make rewards a regular part of your life. Create a list of rewards, both big and small, and use them all along the way as you work to realize your intention.

2. With every project, no matter the size, create a juicy reward for completion of it.

3. Schedule each of the steps for the project and give yourself predetermined rewards for each of the completed steps.

#90   Purpose

Purpose. In the world of theater and film, a director will always challenge their actors to come up with strong objectives for their characters. In other words, it is important for them to be clear about what is the driving force behind all of their actions. In this way, art very much imitates life. What is your life's purpose? What will be the unique way that you have contributed? It is critical to take the time necessary to identify this.

Another way to think of this is by asking yourself the questions "What do you want to do in life and why?" So many people struggle with wondering why they are here on this earth. They feel like they are meant for some greater purpose, but they cannot figure out what it is. However, because they never really take the time to ask these questions and search for the answers, they live lives where they are unfulfilled, and they still have so much left in them to express. Once a person is clear about their purpose and they begin to live it, they immediately experience a level of peace. This peace comes from a knowing that they are in alignment. They have tuned into their spirit and listened to their hearts calling.

One of the biggest principles that must be followed in order to discover your purpose is that it must revolve around something that you are truly passionate about. It must be something that you love. Many mixed emotions come up for most people when they contemplate their existence revolving around doing something that they love. Quite often a person will feel that way of living is just too good to be true—that they don't deserve it. They mistakenly think that they must struggle in order to do well. These concepts that have been picked up from other people are ways of thinking that disconnect you from your purpose. Always remember that joy is your highest and most natural vibration. It is why you are here; your life's work will create that joy for you and others while you do it. Your job is to simply have enough courage, clarity, and feelings of worthiness to declare what it is and fully embrace it.

A great way to shape your purpose is through a mission statement. Have it be concise, a paragraph at max. Your mission statement will be your own personal through line for everything you do, and whenever you are unsure about the best way to go about doing something, simply see what action is most in alignment with your statement. Ask the question "How would I proceed if I were totally embodying my life's purpose?" Your mission statement should include your career or your life's work, but it should also have a code of conduct about who you are and how you want to be even when you are not working. Having this clarity filters through even the simplest of tasks, from a get-together with friends, to a meeting at work, or exercise at the gym. Before you do anything always ask yourself "what is my purpose here?" What do I want to give and get out of this situation? By directing your focus this way, not only will every experience be more gratifying, but you are also assured of turning the movie of your life into a masterpiece.

ACTION STEPS FOR LIVING YOUR LIFE'S PURPOSE

1. Take some time to create your purpose by reflecting on who you are, how you want to be, and what you want to do in life. Then write a mission statement no longer than a paragraph describing it.

2. After you have flushed out your mission statement, then write out your purpose in one sentence. It helps to think of your purpose as a one-line summary of your mission statement.

3. Take at least three minutes daily where you affirm your purpose with as much emotion as you can generate. While you are doing this, reflect on how you are providing service for yourself and others when you are living this purpose.

#91   Role Modeling

Role modeling. "No man or woman is an island." In order to excel, you must build off of other people's knowledge, experience, and understanding. People who feel that they can do it all by themselves usually do not ever realize their full potential. No matter what you do, you can't be a success at it without some kind of help from other people. One of the greatest ways to benefit from the vast sea of information and experience that other people have is by role modeling. It bears repeating that saying "if someone has something you want, then they know something you don't." In this way you must be like a detective, and find those clues that lead to your success. Whatever your goal is, the chances are high that someone else has already done it or at least some aspect of it before.

If you can meet this individual in person or learn about them from a class or book, and then model them, you will be able to shift the odds in your favor. When you take the same steps they took and think the same way they did, there is a strong chance that you will meet with at least some of the same success that they have had. Heed the term "you reap what you sow." If you sow the same seeds, you will reap the same kinds of results.

Probably more than anything else to role model, it is important take note of their mind-set. Remember that "in order to have an extraordinary life, you must have an extraordinary psychology," as Tony Robbins said. How you think and feel are the most important aspects of your success. They are not the only aspects—action is very important as well—but mind-set and feeling come before action. If a person has the right mind-set, then they will naturally take the right actions. Also if a person has the right mind-set, then their consistent actions will eventually bear fruit. It is imperative to remember that in order to manifest anything, you must emit the same vibration as that which you want. In other words, you must act as if you already have your end result because no amount of action can ever make up for misalignment even if you are role modeling a person who is a huge success. The person who has what you want was a vibrational match for what they envisioned before they had it. Everything is energy. Most people are so action-oriented that they ignore the great importance of the vibration that creates the mind-set. This is why many people work very hard with little results. It is because of the right mind-set that the actions work. When role modeling, make it a point to study the seeds that have been planted by these successes and then mirror their qualities of thoughts and feelings as well as actions and then you will give yourself the greatest edge.

ACTION STEPS FOR ROLE MODELING

1. Identify someone who has what you want.

2. Study their mind-set, vibration, and the actions they have taken in order to get them where they are.

3. See if that person could mentor you with the project you are working on. Volunteer your services and give back to your mentor for the valuable information that they will be giving you. If you are not able to do this, then offer to take them to lunch so you can ask them questions. It is also ideal to read any books, listen to any audios, and take any courses on or by that person.

#92   Genius

Genius. Throughout history, there have been a number of geniuses. Many of them are no longer with us, as they are considered legends. However, a select few are very much alive today. They are considered to be the standard bearers for their chosen fields. They are seen as being innovative, creative, and quite often they are extremely accomplished. Another characteristic of these so-called geniuses is that they are seen as being very rare. It is said that they come along once in a blue moon. Let's take a closer look at what makes up a genius. Whereas the above-mentioned qualities are difficult to argue, it must be noted that a major part of what makes a genius stand out is the fact that they are or were exceptionally good at something. However, everyone possesses this God-given gift of unlimited potential. Thomas Edison said, "If we all did the things we are capable of doing, we would literally astound ourselves."

All people, regardless of background, age, or creed, have unique talents. This includes the homeless man on the street and the ninety-year-old woman in a nursing home. The reason geniuses are so rare is because they not only develop their talents, but they also have accessed a greater amount of their resources enabling them to take that talent to unprecedented heights. Edison also said, "Genius is 1 percent inspiration and 90 percent perspiration."

In other words, the genius has consistently tapped into their power, enthusiasm, and focus—all qualities that stem from within. Anyone can do this if these three pieces of the puzzle are consistently in place. Simply determine what areas your special talents are in, spend a lifetime developing them, and figure out the greatest way that they can serve humanity. Nelson Mandela said, "There is no passion to be found in playing small—in settling for a life that is less than what you are capable of living."

Before you can do this, you must understand that you already are a genius. You may not have accomplished all that you have envisioned yet. You may not even know what all your special talents are, but you already have all that you need in order tap into your unique gifts. It is easier to access them if you are able to understand that they are there from the beginning. Your gifts will still need to be developed, but if you know that those seeds were already planted in you when you came into existence, then you no longer have to wonder whether it is possible or if you are worthy of being a genius. Remember what the genius artist Michelangelo said when he built the famous sculpture *David*. When asked how he did it, he replied by saying, "David was already there, I just chipped away at the rough edges." In the same way, your genius is already there; you just need to chip away at the rough edges and fine-tune your gifts so you can share them in the greatest way. The bottom line is that you can never let anyone, including yourself, fool you into thinking that you cannot be a genius, because it is your birthright to be one.

ACTION STEPS FOR REALIZING YOUR GENIUS

1. Acknowledge and understand that you already are a genius and that you must simply make sure that it is fully developed and expressed in this lifetime.

2. Figure out what your special gifts are by paying close attention to what you love to do and may already have a knack for.

3. Spend your entire life developing these gifts by tapping into your power, enthusiasm, and focus and consistently searching for greater ways to serve humanity with them.

#93 Moods

Moods. They parallel the weather with how frequently they change. From being filled with happiness to being drenched with gloom, our moods bounce around like Ping-Pong balls. It's not a question of if our moods will change; it is a matter of when. The tricky thing about them is that most people let these feelings prevent them from taking action on tasks, projects, and ideas that they would ideally follow through on.

Moods are a natural part of the ebb and flow of the human experience. Yet you can actually have a big effect on the moods you regularly experience if you practice thinking from the end and always focus on what you want. Your focus determines what you feel, and your feelings can greatly determine what actions you take. Again, human beings can pretty much only focus on one thought at a time, and 80 percent of your thoughts are habitual. The vast majority of them are the same thoughts that you thought yesterday. If you can train yourself to think such that 80 percent of your thoughts are on what you are creating then not only will you feel better, but you will also realize more of what you envision.

It is important to understand that you cannot experience joy without clearly focusing on what you want. However, there are different variations of this. On a basic level it is good to have the overall intention of always wanting to feel good. As Wayne Dyer said, "Feeling good is the equivalent of feeling God or being connected to your source." This is the energy of creation and the vibration that attracts abundance in life. Yet this energy can be elevated even further if you determine ahead of time what you want each segment of your day to look like. Esther and Jerry Hicks called this process "segment intending." The more you predetermine what you want each block of time in your life to be like, the more you are setting forces in place that help create that situation for you. When you don't predetermine a situation then it is much easier for you to fall prey to random moods or any kind of stimulus from your environment. Therefore, segment intending is one of the best ways to consistently experience great moods.

ACTION STEPS FOR CREATING AND DEALING WITH MOODS

1. Always practice segment intending with every event in your life no matter how big or small because it will consistently create great moods.

2. Never wait for your mood to be perfect before you take action toward a desired result because you will lose precious time. There will never be the perfect mood or situation to begin a project, so start now wherever you are. By taking action you actually begin to get control over your emotions because each step of progress will alleviate negative feelings.

3. Lastly you must understand that your moods will always be shifting and that is natural and that there is nothing wrong with that. Yet you can experience more uplifting ones as you take action, go through meditation and prayer, and simply lighten up and love yourself. The secret is to never try and fight the unwanted mood. It will only grow stronger; instead, let it be and practice segment intending. The more you do this, the more you will see desired results showing up in your life.

#94   Increase Your Value

Increase your value. How much are you worth? Not just in financial terms, but what kind of value do you provide for people? So many people want to make more money in their lives. It has been said that "money is just a measurement for the amount of value that a person brings to the marketplace." There is an unspoken law in life that says in order to grow, you must increase the number of people you touch. In other words if you want to increase the amount of money you make then you must increase not only the quality of what you do but also the quantity of people that you bring value to. Put another way, you must increase your influence. Once you discover what your gift is and the unique way that it is going to make a difference in the world, the question then becomes how can you expand on that gift? How can you grow such that your talents benefit more people? Following this principle creates total synergy in one's life; it forces you to grow, which then enables you to contribute on a greater scale. When this happens, the ripple effect is tremendous. Because you have increased your influence, your work becomes more valuable.

As a result, you'll be attracting more abundance and prosperity into your life. Your spirit will be content as you fulfill your purpose and meet the needs of countless others as well. The richest people in the world not only do what they love to do, but they also serve the greatest number of people. There is an old saying in business that goes, "people don't care how much you know, until they know how much you care." It is when we focus on living a life of service that all of the pieces in the puzzle fall into place. When we are consumed by petty details and lose sight of our overall purpose then we fall out of sync with the universe. Conversely when our energies are directed toward the giving of ourselves, we find that we end up attracting every kind of reward imaginable. Wayne Dyer put it beautifully when he said, "If a person's focus is always on what's in it for me then they will constantly have that reflected back to them, but when a person's energy is on how may I serve, then the universe will reflect that energy back to them and always be serving them."

ACTION STEPS FOR INCREASING YOUR VALUE

1. Determine to live a life of service where you give your life away.

2. Get clear on what your unique contribution is to the world and then spend your life developing those gifts.

3. With regards to business, remember that as you consistently create more and more value for people, you will create more and more wealth and abundance in your own life.

#95   Be Unreasonable

Be unreasonable. Have you ever stopped to notice that cynics and skeptics never achieve anything above mediocrity? It is always the dreamers who seemingly realize miracles. The so-called legends who we read about and have statues made in their image are never the individuals who say something can't be done. They are never the kind of people who are filled with doubt and just go along with the masses. Unreasonable people rule the world. Anais Nin said, "Life shrinks and expands in proportion to one's courage." The point here is that a person with an average life lives within the confines of their immediate circumstances, whereas the extraordinary individual creates their own circumstances.

In order to live the life of your dreams, you must be unreasonable. This does not mean that you lose perspective and don't use logic. It means that you think and act outside of the box. In order to do this, you have to be in touch with your inner self and have the courage to listen to its guidance. Again, meditation and prayer are powerful tools in quieting the mind and hearing the inner voice, because quite often it whispers.

Perhaps the biggest challenge with being unreasonable is having the strength of character to deal with other people's opinion of you. Many people tend to judge or feel threatened when they see someone else living in alignment with their inner guide. For them it can be a painful reminder of how they are not listening to their own guidance, and because they are not ready to grow and do this in their own lives, they resent the messenger. Instead of adopting an empowering mind-set and being inspired by your example, they are angered by this reflection. Even though at times this can be challenging to deal with, it must be noted that the best way to support these people is for you to shine your light. No amount of poverty, struggle, sickness, or lack of fulfillment on your part will ever uplift them. Your duty is to make sure that you live your purpose to the fullest so that the people who are ready to be served by it can benefit.

It cannot be stated enough that when you listen to your intuition and follow through despite fear and other people's opinions, you experience miracles in your life, and these miracles can end up having a profound effect on humanity. The more unreasonable you are, the more you open up your world to endless possibility. Every great feat or invention began in the mind first. So when you get the urge to do something that goes against the grain of what people say can be done, make a decision to listen to that urge and be unreasonable. George Bernard Shaw stated it beautifully: "The reasonable man adopts himself to the world; the unreasonable one persists in trying to adapt the world to himself. Therefore, all progress depends on the unreasonable man."

ACTION STEPS TO BE UNREASONABLE

1. Embrace the idea of being unreasonable as a necessary component for the full expression of your purpose.

2. Practice being unreasonable by consistently taking calculated risks that strengthen your courage and stretch your comfort zone.

3. Bless and send love to people who are threatened by your ways, and continue to shine while keeping your distance from them as much as possible.

#96 Trust

Trust. This is one of the greatest qualities a person can have. It is a key ingredient to manifesting your dreams and living a life of peace. Trust means that you are able conduct yourself with an absence of doubt. It means your faith in the final outcome is so strong that your trust in the universe's support is unshakable. Despite whatever setbacks that may pop up, you are clear that you will realize your vision. Trust is extremely important because it will aid in attracting the desired result. Being that like attracts like, this principle must be understood by anyone who wants to create something in their life.

The way to truly internalize this understanding is to act as if the desired result is already your reality now in the present moment. This may feel a bit awkward at first because it may seem that your current reality is so far away from where you want to be. However, this is the perfect time to embrace this principle. Remember, if everyone had to have physically done something before they could have confidence or trust about it, then no one would ever accomplish anything above mediocrity. You must be a vibrational match with what you desire or you will not have it. In most cases you will literally have to make believe or pretend for a while before you are able to totally act as if. Yet you must have trust in order to even practice living your life in this way because this kind of mental conditioning can take awhile. Therefore, your ideal results may also take a while. Yet as you consistently take the actions that are in alignment with your vision and add as much positive emotion and expectation to everything you do, eventually you will fully believe, and the universe will reward you for your trust.

Psychologists have done significant studies that have found that people with very clear and definitive visions of themselves, who act as if they are already where they desire to be, end up ultimately getting there the vast majority of the time. As Goethe said, "The moment one definitely commits oneself, then providence moves too. All sorts of things occur to help one that would never otherwise have occurred. A whole stream of events issues from the decision raising in one's favor all manner of unforeseen incidents and meetings and material assistance, which no one could have dreamed would have come their way. Whatever you can do, or dream you can begin it. Boldness has genius, power and magic in it. Begin it now."

ACTION STEPS TO EXPERIENCE TRUST

1. Whatever it is that you want in your life—a big raise, a great relationship, fun at your job—trust that you can and will have it.

2. Demonstrate this trust to yourself and the universe by keeping your mind's attention on the intended outcome regardless of the outside circumstances. Act as if all you desire is already a fact in your life. Feel the feelings that you would if you already had exactly what you want.

3. Plan out and take all the actions necessary to position yourself to receive the desired result. Make the necessary adjustments to your plan as needed and never give up. As you do this, make sure that your words and actions of certainty surpass any doubt that enters your mind. Once you can do this and stick to it so that it becomes routine, you have won the game and it is just a matter of time before you get it.

#97 Detachment

Detachment. Practicing detachment can feel a bit like an out-of-body experience, because most people live in a world that is primarily based on just the opposite. Embracing this principle can have you feel like you are from another planet because you may often find yourself surrounded by people who don't operate this way and cannot understand how it is even possible. Most people are attached to what other people think, say, and do. They are attached to the results of their efforts and those of others. They are attached to the appearance of things and the meanings they have given to them. There is attachment everywhere.

The problem is that attachment blocks you. It impedes your connection to the universal flow—that energy that comes from your highest self. It prevents you from being fully self-expressed and having the freedom to be. Attachment limits the degree of success and happiness that you can experience because you are dependent on others for the permission to have it. Even if you are taking effective action, if you are overly attached to the results, then the amount of joy you can experience is severely limited by those results. This means you can only experience peace and happiness when you have everything turn out exactly the way you want it. This can happen, but it often takes a certain amount of adjustment in your thoughts and actions before it does, and since "correcting and continuing" is such a large part of being successful, it is important to be happy while you are doing it. Quite often attachment can prevent you from even following through on your vision because you may lose your faith. If you don't see results when you think they should show up, it is easy to quit.

Conversely, detachment demonstrates a trust in the universe and ourselves that opens up the pathways to success. Detachment enables you to release others from your agendas as you take responsibility for the things you can control and let go with the things you can't. Detachment is one of the greatest gifts that you can give yourself, because it connects you to love. This love that stems from within is unconditional. It does not depend on a certain result to be given. It is the very source that links everything together, including your ability to create your destiny. When you are in tune with it, the universe, by law of attraction, reflects that love back to you and creates support and opportunities to realize your intentions.

ACTION STEPS FOR DETACHMENT

1. In making your commitment to detachment, be clear that at times it may be challenging because you are strengthening a muscle that most people do not use.

2. With every project, situation, and goal you have, clearly intend the outcome.

3. If something does not play out the way you would ideally like, continue to stay focused on your vision. Then joyfully make any necessary adjustments while trusting in the universe to help you realize that intention or something better.

#98   Being Right

Being right. If there is one thing that is the death of most human relationships, including your relationship with yourself, it is the need to be right. This disease of the mind is the fuel that enables the ego to burn. When you are stuck in "rightville," your thoughts, words, and actions are cut off from love. Instead, they come from a need to prove yourself. Being right is one of the strongest impulses of the ego. Many people would rather die than to admit they are wrong. As a result they can spend their whole life trying to validate themselves by making other people wrong. When you function in this way, you cannot fully be at peace.

Remember, peace is what the spirit ultimately wants. Yet in order to have it, you must generate unconditional love. This means that you are able to exist free of the need to prove. It does not mean that you can't accomplish miracles that other people doubt are possible; it means that your way of being is a result of purpose that stems from unconditional love and the desire to use your gifts to serve humanity.

The terms "right" and "wrong" can be very rigid labels that people impose on one another. Awareness of right and wrong is not simply referring to a bunch of moral rules. In a more holistic sense, it is about your capacity to acknowledge when a certain way of being with your thoughts and actions does not serve you or the situation. When you have this awareness and make the necessary adjustments to be in alignment with your intention for peace, then you will naturally experience a higher level in your life.

It is when you are able to reach this Zen-like place that you are truly at your greatest; otherwise, when you are busy being right, you may accomplish things, but there is never total self-fulfillment because you are harnessing anger, resentment, or a need to compensate where you feel you are lacking. It is in this way that being right can actually be quite wrong. This way of being sucks the joy out of life. As the saying goes, "you can be right, or you can be in love." This applies not only to romantic relationships but also to your relationship to yourself and the world. As Wayne Dyer said, "When you have the opportunity to be right or to be kind, choose kindness." This will have you feel good, and as the saying goes, to "feel good is to feel God." In other words, when you live based on the guidance of your higher purpose, you experience true lightness of being and consequently live a life that is beyond your greatest dreams.

ACTION STEPS FOR TRULY BEING RIGHT

1. Forget about proving yourself to others and understand that truly being right means thinking and doing in ways that bring you joy and peace.

2. In your personal relationships, when you are faced with a choice to be right or to be kind, be kind.

3. Listen to your spirit and follow its guidance with every single decision in your life.

#99   You Get What You Give

You get what you give. Consider that your life is the way it is because of the choices you have made. On a deeper level, consider that you receive from life what you give to it. This principle works in a couple of different ways. The harder you work and the more energy that you put into something, the greater your chances of success. This cause and effect is a law of the universe.

Yet what is less known about this principle is that it also works karmically—"every action has an equal reaction." Everything you do is an offering to the world. As Richard Carlson, PhD, says, "Nature returns whatever offerings it is given with interest." Some possible ways to apply this understanding are as follows. If you want more love in your life, give more love. Even if your return does not come back from the person you gave it to, trust that it will come back to you in some way. If you want more money in your life, give some away. If you want more happiness, trust, or inspiration or anything else, simply give it away. There is a saying that Les Brown used that goes "you can't spray perfume on somebody else without getting a few drops on yourself." As a rule of thumb, whatever it is you would like to see showing up in your life, give it away first because we don't get what we want, we get what we are. You must be the vibrational match to whatever it is that you want.

The other qualities that must be in place after you do this are detachment and patience. They are significant because they free you up to be connected to your purpose and release your fears while moving through any obstacles. Do not look for the universe to immediately give you back whatever it is you gave, because then you are only giving so you can receive. When you operate out of this agenda, all that you do is conditional. In order to realize your vision, you must give unconditionally with no strings attached. As you do this, you will have the trust that all of your divine good will manifest itself in due time, and there are no demands on the universe if it does not meet your timetable. Quite often, by detaching in this way, your good comes back to you faster than you could have imagined because you are not blocking it with your emotions.

ACTION STEPS FOR GETTING WHAT YOU GIVE

1. Constantly ask yourself the question "How may I serve?"

2. Use the golden rule for guidance and think about how you would like to be treated when considering how to treat others. Even more specifically, regularly ask the question "How would this other person like me to treat them?"

3. Share everything out of love, while being one with your highest self. When you do this, you will naturally experience whatever you are giving away, and it will spontaneously come back to you multiplied.

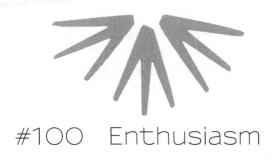

#100   Enthusiasm

Enthusiasm. This is one of the greatest traits a person can possess. One who exudes it can accomplish anything. The very word enthusiasm stems from the Greek term *enthios*, which means "filled with God." With such strong roots, it's easy to see how enthusiasm can be so powerful. The thing about this special force is that it is contagious.

Contrary to what many think, enthusiasm does not require that you be yelling and screaming about what you are engaged in. It simply means that you are passionate about what you're doing. That passion can express itself through words, actions, thoughts, or all of the above.

No matter what the intention, enthusiasm creates enrollment. It makes no difference whether a person is negative or positive; if they have this quality they will have a profound effect on those in their field of influence. Throughout history the most powerful people have had intense enthusiasm that enabled them to lead many people.

Since we all have this quality, it is only a matter of cultivating it. When we are in touch with our highest self and are clear about our purpose, it comes naturally. The most powerful way to channel this energy is when you are using it to empower yourself and others. Put simply, when you use enthusiasm to uplift and serve humanity, you truly align with your source and become most powerful. Your influence suddenly not only reaches beyond your grasp, but also feels good when you share it. If you are meticulous with every action and diligent with each task, then your enthusiasm will automatically build a ladder of success for you. Each successful act will have you attract even more success. Swami Chidvilasananda said of enthusiasm, "Do not judge whether what you are doing is impressive or mediocre, spiritual or mundane. Just do it with enthusiasm. Just do it with this full knowledge: 'God is within me. All actions that I perform are an offering to God.'" As you fine-tune this skill, your enthusiasm will reach new heights, and your accomplishments will reflect this higher level.

ACTION STEPS FOR ENTHUSIASM

1. Let enthusiasm course through you as an offering to the great creator by demonstrating excellence with every single act no matter how big or small.

2. Practice projecting enthusiasm by reading out loud for five minutes a day with as much energy and exuberance as you can muster. This exercise will enable you to turn up your energy on call and give you practice at projecting your purpose.

3. Cultivate the feeling of enthusiasm by constantly maintaining a peak state and engaging in activities that bring you joy.

#101   Love

Love. We have saved the best for last. Love is absolutely, positively, the most powerful force in the universe. We all have an endless supply of it. Its energy brings about tremendous joy to the heart of both the giver and receiver. It is what gives us the courage to move on. It is what supports us with growth and stretching beyond our comfort zone. It is what enables us to reach the greatest heights in our relationships, our work, and our play. It frees our spirit. It gives our life purpose. It lifts our burdens.

For the person who really understands this, the world is their oyster. The strength of love is unparalleled. It is stronger than doubt, stronger than fear, stronger than worry, anger, disbelief, and anxiety. When these emotions confront love, they will always lose. If you were to put love in a competition with hate, love would win every time. Remember when you bring light to dark, the dark can no longer exist. Wayne Dyer's book, *There Is a Spiritual Solution to Every Problem*, touches on this. People so often wonder how to solve their problems. The answer always starts with love. Dyer said, "Whatever the problem, love is the answer." Someone hearing this may say, "Love won't pay the bills" or "Love is not going to get me a new home," but love will put in place the proper energy for you to be able to find the answers, take the action, create the plan, attract the help, expect the best, appreciate the gift in the challenge, embrace the challenge, grow yourself so that you are bigger than the problem, clearly define your purpose, make the adjustments, be a model for what is possible, and simply be a person who constantly gets more in alignment with their purpose with every single situation, and therefore, you are able to serve at the highest level.

Remember that like attracts like. The more you are present to the love within you and the universe, the more you will simply attract more situations to experience that love. This includes all the solutions for your challenges and all the answers to your prayers for guidance.

This can be a challenging energy to stay connected to because we are socialized to approach life from a competitive mind-set instead of a creative one. However, this way of thinking, being, and acting is the root of so many problems because it is moved by ego instead of love. In order to be truly rich in every sense of the word, you must stay connected to feelings of abundance, also known as feelings of love. In short, love is the answer for all good things. Oprah Winfrey said, "Happiness is never something you get from other people. The happiness you feel is in direct proportion to the love you give."

Each day, celebrate love, and give this gift not only to those who expect it, but also to those who don't. Remember to love yourself by going within and by honoring your highest aspirations, for you cannot truly love another until you love yourself first. Love is the be-all and end-all. When you filter love through everything you do, you never have to fear whether things will work out, because you will automatically be a magnet for the best, which is what you deserve. Use the power of love to experience your vast potential, to serve humanity, to realize all of your dreams, and to be happy. It is your privilege. It is your birthright. It is the greatest gift you could ever give to yourself and to the world.

Action Steps for Love

1. Decide to live your life as an agent of love. Pour love into every thought, feeling, and action you can.

2. Regarding other people and any interaction with them, use the golden rule as your guide and only "treat people the way you would have them treat you."

3. Love yourself first by being your own best friend and "treat yourself like a precious object because it will make you strong," as Julia Cameron said. This is important because you cannot give what you don't have.

4. Use the power tools of meditation, journaling, visualization, and affirmation daily to fan this feeling of love every day.

5. Discover what you love to do, and figure out how you can make a living from it. Then leave a legacy that is legendary by using these gifts to serve humanity for the rest of your life.

Appendix A

In order to support you with being able to have amazing success with integrating these 101 secrets from this book, we are giving you a free bonus of your "Wish Fulfilled" complimentary coaching session. This is an extremely empowering session that you won't want to miss. The intention of the session is to create clarity, uncover hidden obstacles, and generate unstoppable momentum to reach your goals.

In your personal one on one session your coach will give you some empowering principles where you will definitely want to take notes because you will truly be getting some very powerful, life changing information. In the second part of the session we will give you some coaching so you can get a sense of our style and how our coaching works. Lastly we will answer any questions you have and break down our various structures so that you can see how the work will empower you to get the results you envision. So if you are interested, call now because space is limited, and these sessions tend to fill up very quickly. May all your wishes come true.

Sincerely, "The Genie"

To set up your free "Wish Fulfilled"
coaching session simply call us at 718-897-2949
or email us at yourwishfulfilled@inneraccess.net

This offer is subject to change or terminate at any time.